Valleys of the Shadow

Valleys of the Shadow

The Memoir of Confederate Captain Reuben G. Clark,
Company I, 59th Tennessee Mounted Infantry

Edited, with Commentary and Regimental History,
by Willene B. Clark

Voices of the Civil War Series
Frank L. Byrne, Series Editor

The University of Tennessee Press • Knoxville

 The Voices of the Civil War Series makes available a variety of primary source materials that illuminate issues on the battlefield, the homefront, and the western front, as well as other aspects of this historic era. The series contextualizes the personal accounts within the framework of the latest scholarship and expands established knowledge by offering new perspectives, new materials, and new voices.

 Copyright © 1994 by The University of Tennessee Press / Knoxville.
All Rights Reserved. Manufactured in the United States of America.
Cloth: First printing, 1994.
Paper: First printing, 2012.

Frontispiece. Reuben Grove Clark (1833–1900), about 1860. Photograph from the editor.

LIBRARY OF CONGRESS CATALOGING IN PUBLICATION DATA

Clark, Reuben G. (Reuben Grove), 1833–1900
  Valleys of the shadow: the memoir of Confederate Captain Reuben G. Clark, Company I, 59th Tennessee Mounted Infantry / edited, with commentary and regimental history, by Willene B. Clark. —1st ed.
    p. cm. — (Voices of the Civil War)
    Includes bibliographical references (p.) and index.
    ISBN 10: 1-57233-529-7
    ISBN 13: 978-1-57233-529-5
  1. Clark, Reuben G. (Reuben Grove), 1833–1900.
  2. United States—History—Civil War, 1861–1865—Prisoners and prisons.
  3. United States—History—Civil War, 1861–1865—Personal narratives.
  4. Prisoners of war—Tennessee—Knoxville—Biography.
  5. Confederate States of America. Army. Tennessee Infantry Regiment, 59th.
  6. Shenandoah Valley Campaign, 1864 (May–August)—Personal narratives.
  7. Knoxville (Tenn.)—Biography.
  I. Clark, Willene B. II. Title. III. Series
  E615.C57   1994
  973.7'82—dc20
  [B]   93-28758
                          CIP

For Karl Gustav Reuben

and Anna Josephine Clark

Contents

Foreword *Frank L. Byrne* ix
Preface xi
Introduction xvi

THE CIVIL WAR EXPERIENCE OF CAPTAIN REUBEN G. CLARK

Chapter 1   5
Chapter 2   8
Chapter 3   11
Chapter 4   23
Chapter 5   26
Chapter 6   30
Chapter 7   50
Chapter 8   53
Chapter 9   68

Epilogue   77
Appendix: The Fifty-ninth Tennessee Mounted Infantry and Company I   85
Notes   115
Bibliography   151
Index   159

Illustrations

Figures
1. "Daisy Dell," Home of the Grove Family, Grainger County, Tennessee   xix
2. Knoxville, Gay Street, with Cowan and Dickinson Store 1869   xxi
3. William G. "Parson" Brownlow   xxv
4. Knoxville County Jail in 1866   xxvii
5. An Iron Cage in the Knoxville County Jail   xxix
6. Munson's Hill, Virginia   13
7. Colonel (later Brigadier General) Alexander W. Reynolds   15
8. Confederate Battery at Vicksburg   17
9. U.S.S. *Hartford*, Flagship of Admiral David G. Farragut   19
10. U.S.S. *Switzerland* and U.S.S. *Lancaster* under Confederate Fire at Vicksburg   20
11. Brigadier General John C. Vaughn   28
12. Major General John C. Breckinridge   32
13. Lieutenant General Jubal A. Early   33
14. Federal Troops Burning in the Shenandoah Valley   34
15. Confederate Forces Crossing the Potomac in 1862   35
16. Sheridan's Army in the Shenandoah   37
17. Cavalry Action at the Battle of Third Winchester   39
18. Fisher's Hill, Virginia   40
19. Confederate Troops at Martinsburg, Virginia   45
20. Confederate Troops at Hagerstown, Maryland   47
21. Dr. Charles Leonard, Tenth Michigan Cavalry, USA   63
22. Knoxville County Court House   71
23. Reuben G. Clark, about 1894   78
24. Mary Josephine ("Daisy") King Clark, about 1894   79
25. "Belle Vue," the Clark home in Rome, Georgia   81

Maps
1. East Tennessee   xiii
2. The Mississippi Valley in the Area of Vicksburg   xiv
3. The Shenandoah Valley   xv

Foreword

This memoir is the inaugural volume of the University of Tennessee Press's Voices of the Civil War Series, which brings to twentieth-century readers the words of contemporaries of America's greatest war. While the series includes people of all kinds, it especially aims to amplify the voices of ignored and marginalized individuals and groups. One such man was Reuben G. Clark, an East Tennessean who, unlike most East Tennesseans, belonged to the minority willing to fight for the Confederacy. His recollections give the other side of Tennessee's bitter domestic conflict.

As a Confederate, Clark served as a company officer of the Fifty-ninth Tennessee Mounted Infantry. He describes minor skirmishes and great battles, such as those of the Vicksburg Campaign. Especially rich in human-interest detail is his narrative of fighting and flirting in the Shenandoah Valley in 1864, with some new information on the battle of Piedmont. Willene B. Clark, the editor of this volume, has identified people mentioned by Clark (her grandfather) and supplied background for his observations. In addition, she has written an appendix that provides a valuable summary of the unit's war service, thus filling another of the many gaps in the ranks of Confederate regimental histories.

With his capture in East Tennessee late in 1864, Clark begins the most important part of his memoir. He was imprisoned in a cage in the Knoxville Jail under false charges of murder publicized by William

G. "Parson" Brownlow. His sufferings compare precisely with those of Tennessee Unionists previously held in the same place. His narrative of his subsequent prosecution for treason and of the enforcement of the Confiscation Act is a rare record of forgotten legal proceedings. As he shows, hatred and even violence among Tennesseans did not end with the war. Self-exiled to Rome, Georgia, Clark succeeded in businesses that doubtless pleased the advocates of a New South. Happily for us, he also joined his voice in the reminiscent chorus of the Civil War's veterans.

Frank L. Byrne
Kent State University

Preface

As a child I was thrilled by the tales in my grandfather's Civil War memoir, preserved in a slim typescript volume bound in red leather and kept on a shelf in the den. It brought to life a man who died when my father was only two years old, but whose handsome face was familiar to me in the portrait my mother drew of him from a photograph. Now, after many years of teaching as an art historian, I have turned again to the memoir, this time to present it in a critical edition, as a rare example of an East Tennessean's firsthand account of the Civil War.

The most fruitful source of information about the Tennesseans referred to in the memoir is the Calvin M. McClung Historical Collection of the East Tennessee Historical Center in Knoxville. I am grateful for help from the McClung Collection director, Steve Cotham, members of his staff, and Knoxville historian Pollyanna Creekmore. Family members have made many contributions: Mary King Battey, Josephine Battey Hollingworth, Gary Clark, Holland Ball Clark, John Miller Clark, John Grove Peck, and Mary Cooper Smith. For a variety of documents and information, I am indebted to Jacqueline D. Kinzer of the Rome-Floyd County Library (Rome, Georgia); Dr. C. J. Wyatt of Rome; Arthur Wagner of the Tennessee State Library and Archives; Marion O. Smith of the Andrew Johnson Project of the University of Tennessee; Lynda Crist of the Papers of Jefferson Davis of Rice University; the Virginia Department of Historic Resources;

Michael Musick of the National Archives; Mary Ann Hawkins of the National Archives, Southeastern Region; Edwin C. Bearss, Office of History and Historic Architecture of the National Park Service, and Terrence J. Winschel, National Park Service; the Virginia State Library and Archives (Richmond, Virginia); the Maryland Historical Society; the Washington County (Maryland) Historical Society (Hagerstown, Maryland); the Handley Library (Winchester, Virginia); and for help with problems in American studies, Regina Blaszczyk and Richard M. Judd, and in military history, Ross D. Netherton and Mark Stoller. I am grateful to Lewis L. Gould and Jeffry D. Wert, as well as Marlboro College colleagues and friends Eyre H. Davisson, Richard M. Judd, and Timothy Little, for reading the typescript and offering excellent suggestions for its improvement; and to Professor Gould for making me aware of several primary source documents. I owe a special debt to the University of Tennessee Press's readers for the impetus to explore the military aspects of the memoir and for their helpful suggestions and corrections. The Marlboro College Library staff members were tireless in their efforts to locate and obtain research materials for me.

Willene B. Clark
Marlboro College

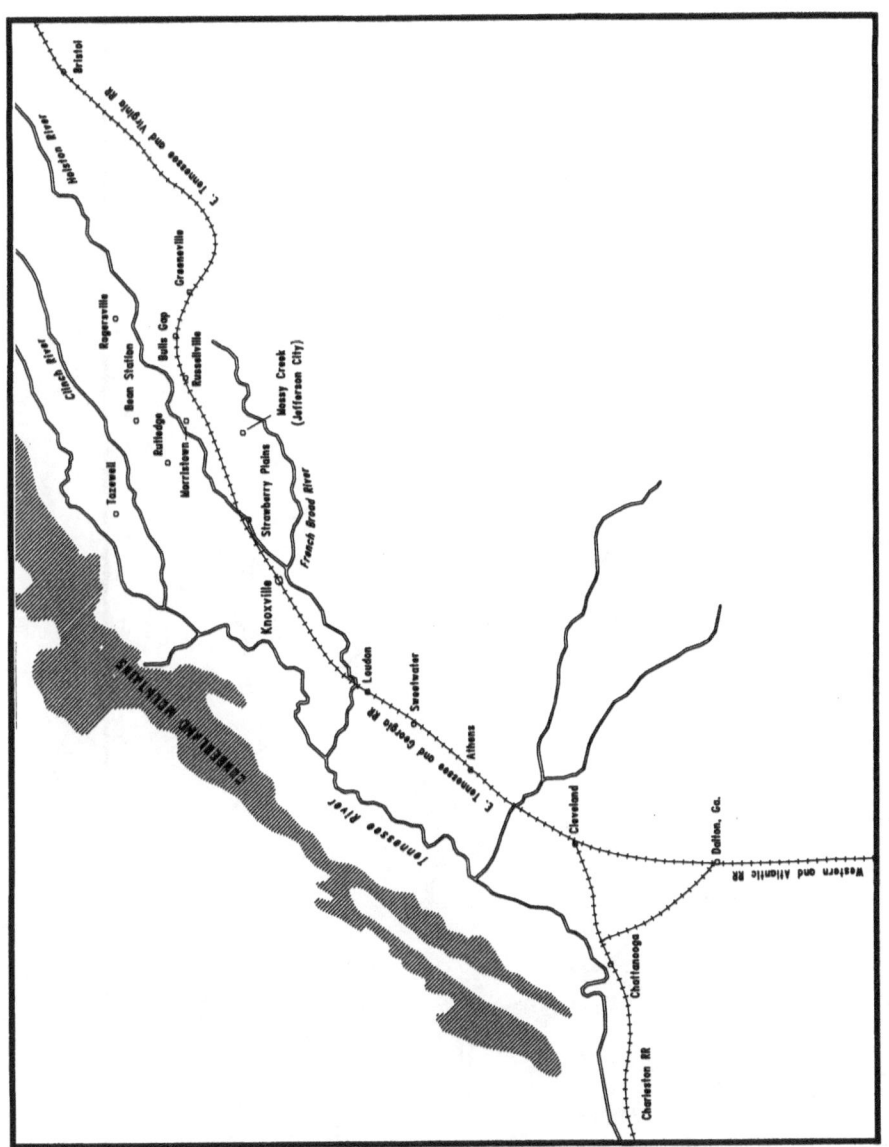

Map 1. East Tennessee. Map by David Goodwin.

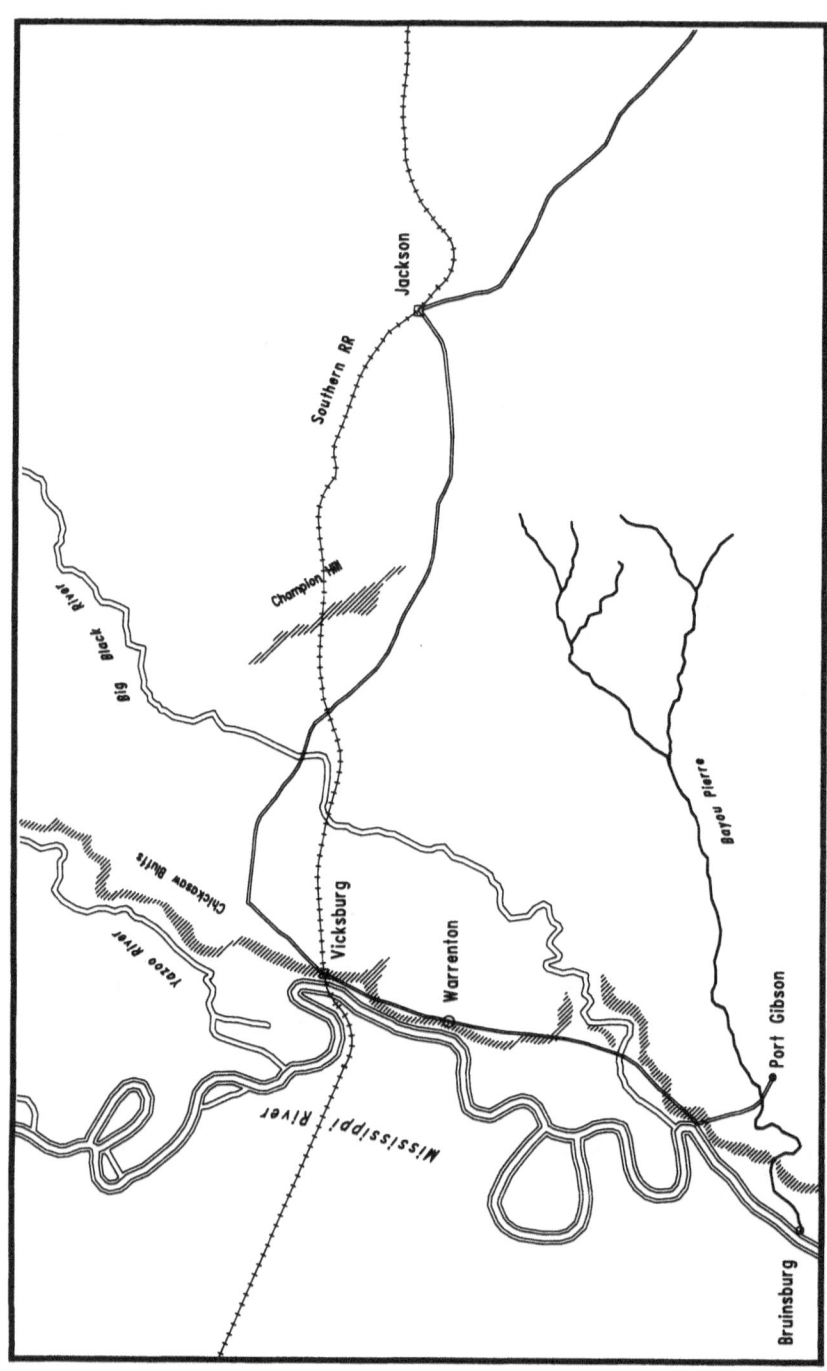

Map 2. The Mississippi Valley in the area of Vicksburg. Map by David Goodwin.

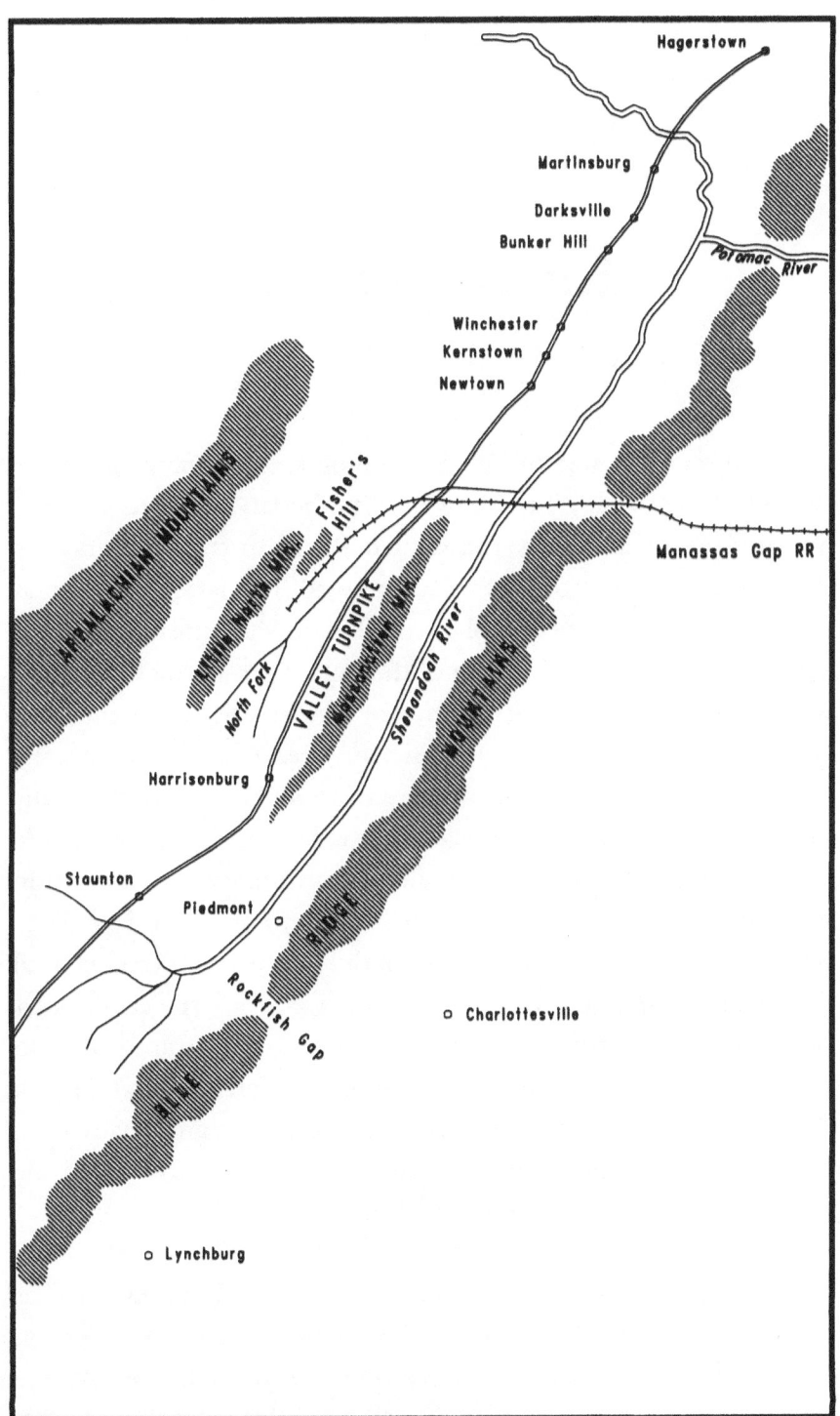

Map 3. The Shenandoah Valley. Map by David Goodwin.

Introduction

East Tennessee is an area of hills and rolling agricultural lands in the great Appalachian Valley, framed by the Cumberland and Great Smoky Mountains, and watered by the Clinch River to the west and the Holston and French Broad rivers to the east. The latter two join at Knoxville, the region's principal city, to become the great Tennessee River that courses through much of the state. During the first half of the nineteenth century, East Tennessee was isolated from the burgeoning industrialism that occurred in many areas of the United States. Narrow passes through the two ranges of mountains, and rivers unsuited to heavy commercial navigation made links to national trade and supply routes difficult.[1] As a result, pre-war industry in the region was sparse and relatively light.[2] Railroads did not come to East Tennessee until the 1850s, and the first train did not reach Knoxville until 1855. The meat animals, horses, and mules that were the area's principal exports were driven to markets in the Carolinas and south to Georgia and Alabama on the turnpike across Clinch Mountain, north of Knoxville. With an economy based on family farms and small shops, rather than on large plantations, there were few slave owners in the region, and they owned but a few slaves.

While the central and western parts of the state looked primarily to the South, East Tennesseans tended to identify themselves less as Southerners than as Tennesseans and Americans, so when secession came, the loyalties of many in the region were to the Union. As one writer remarked recently, they "saw little future in joining a rebellion of southern states in which they had little at stake and much to lose."[3] Yet there were those East Tennesseans who thought of the South as their homeland, and although many were Unionists at heart, they gave their support to the Confederacy. The larger landowners—the gentry—were the most likely to side with the Confederacy, for they felt more akin to the plantation South than did the subsistence farmers.[4]

As a result of these peculiar economic conditions and the varying allegiances in East Tennessee, no part of the nation saw deeper divisions or more bitter hatreds in its populace. Neither the cool green of the valleys nor the mountain snows could damp the fiery enmities that arose among East Tennesseans when Governor Isham G. Harris joined the state's military forces to the Confederacy on June 8, 1861. Until late August 1863 the region was under what an antagonistic majority of citizens considered a Confederate "occupation." On September 1, however, amid the tumultuous cheers of the loyalists, Union troops under Major General Ambrose Burnside entered and took charge of Knoxville.[5] Both the Confederate and Federal administrations participated in an endless spectacle of harassment, arrests, killings, and property appropriation and destruction against East Tennessee civilians of the opposite camp. So acrimonious were the political disagreements and so deeply entrenched the hatreds resulting from real or perceived atrocities committed on both sides, that mutual distrust and ill will lasted in East Tennessee for many years after the war.[6]

It was here, on a farm in Grainger County, that the author of this Civil War memoir was born and raised, and here that he enlisted in the Confederate service in 1861. Despite the violent divisions of his homeland and his allegiance to the Confederacy, he remained sensible of his kinship with those he was forced to call his enemies. He felt deeply the rifts that the war created between families, friends, and neighbors, but he also saw that, in East Tennessee as elsewhere, there were people on both sides for whom the tragedy of the war overshadowed the loyalties, and who looked ahead toward peace and reconciliation.

Confederate Captain Reuben Grove Clark wrote his memoir in 1891, over a quarter-century after the war. Although he claimed in the dedication that the work was not intended to entertain, he organized his material in discrete chapters and paced his story for dramatic effect, pausing at times in the action to increase the reader's anticipation of a crisis or resolution. He is a good storyteller, yet there are often passages in his narrative that beg for a richer perspective than he provided. In the first half of his book, almost as a prelude, Clark recalls the main events of his combat experiences, sometimes offering heretofore unknown facts. The second part is the heart of the story, his physical and legal struggles during eight months as a prisoner of war in Knoxville, the town that had become his home. At the end he provides fascinating glimpses into the tensions that Confederate soldiers often faced in East Tennessee after the war and describes court proceedings for which detailed records are now lost.

Reuben Clark (1833–1900) was born November 10 on a farm near Rutledge, Tennessee, in a mountainous area northeast of Knoxville, the son of Joseph Clark (1800–65) and his second wife, Martha Grove Clark (1812–96).[7] In the late 1820s Joseph held the office of Justice of the Peace in Grainger County, and on the 1832 county tax list he is recorded as the owner of 128 acres of farm land, for the period a respectable but not a large holding.[8] Joseph lived with his wife and children in a log house, the most common type of structure in the region at that time.[9] Log houses built by farmers of comfortable means, such as Joseph Clark, had one and a half or two stories and a single chimney. His in-laws, the Groves, were well-to-do and like other wealthy planters built a two-story frame house with siding and two chimneys (fig. 1). Most East Tennessee farmers, including the Clarks and the Groves, were not slave owners, but worked the land themselves with the help of one or two young people who are listed in census records along with family members.[10] Most settlers in East Tennessee were of English and Irish/Scottish stock, and many, like the Clarks, were Presbyterians.[11] During the war, Reuben's company and his regiment were made up of men and boys from these unpretentious families that lived quietly and tilled their own soil.

Fig. 1. "Daisy Dell," home of the Grove family, Grainger County, Tennessee. Photograph courtesy of John Grove Peck.

The memoir provides only a glimpse of Reuben Clark's life before the war. He spent his childhood on the family farm, working regularly in the fields during growing and harvesting seasons. He raised at least one pig, which he sold for travel money when he left home to seek his fortune. His formal education was both intermittent and insufficient. The little school he attended on his father's property and the inept teachers he encountered there are typical of the education provided in those days in the rural counties of Tennessee.[12] A member of his military company, William J. Kirkham, also of Grainger County, stated in a post-war interview that "almost every large farm or plantation had its school-house. Usually of logs and with fireplaces for the burning of wood."[13] Kirkham added that it was customary for parents to pay the teacher one dollar per month for each pupil. Reuben was sixteen when he left both school and home to join his half-brother Samuel in a small store in Rutledge, the county seat. He worked the first year for board and clothing, the second for the annual sum of $150.[14] When Samuel left for Missouri, Reuben worked in a nearby town for a time, then tried unsuccessfully to obtain more education. His lack of proper training is occasionally reflected in his prose constructions, yet overall his writing is logical, often imaginative, and well organized.

Reuben was an ambitious youth, and despite his poor education, was successful in his first serious business venture. Leaving Grainger County in about 1852, he went to Knoxville, where he obtained a position at Cowan and Dickinson, a wholesale-retail dry goods and grocery establishment that was one of the most important commercial firms in the state (fig. 2).[15] At the time, Knoxville proper had a population of just under six thousand people, but with its neighboring villages, could probably count the eight thousand Clark mentions. Throughout its early history, Knoxville, like the whole region, was isolated from the broader lines of commerce and manufacturing, and at mid-century it was therefore smaller than Nashville, the state capitol, and than the Mississippi River city of Memphis; it was about the same size as Chattanooga. In addition to the usual retail trade of a regional center, Knoxville was known for export production of livestock for meat, as well as horses and mules for farm work. With the advent of rail service to Knoxville in 1855, manufacturing began to grow.[16] Reuben saw a bright future in the city, with its potential for importance beyond East Tennessee, and set about to master the skills required by his employer, business skills that would serve him well in his post-war career. He became acquainted, both socially and in business, with leading citizens of the city and of the region, some of whom would later be crucial to his very survival. By 1860 he was living in the home of Frank H. McClung, a prominent merchant of Knoxville, whose son is mentioned in the memoir as one of Reuben's best friends.[17]

The Clarks were Whigs, and to judge by the views Reuben expresses in his text, they must have subscribed to the Unionist rather than the states' rights wing of the party.[18] Reuben writes that he, his

Fig. 2. Knoxville, Gay Street, with Cowan and Dickinson store in right foreground, 1869. Photograph courtesy of the McClung Historical Collection, Knoxville.

father, and his brother were active in supporting political candidates in various elections, traveling with them and speaking on their behalf. Political activity gave him further access to influential circles in East Tennessee. He thoroughly enjoyed the social whirl of Knoxville, and his awareness of his position as a "gentleman" was typical of upper-class Southerners of the period.[19] This class consciousness is reflected in the chivalric code of honor exhibited in the memoir, a code that prevented Clark at one point from fleeing prison, and even possible execution, because he would not betray a trust. But his social position also put him in great danger at the end of the war, for it was the gentry who were most vilified by the victorious Unionists of East Tennessee. A letter in *The Knoxville Whig and Rebel Ventilator* for May 17, 1865, asks, "Is our community to be kept in constant commotion by the swaggering airs of the *aristocratic* young gentlemen who, in former days, were ever ready to shoot Union men . . . ? It may be better for returning rebels to travel on a little further." The letter is signed "An East Tennessean."[20]

Reuben Clark boasts that he worked hard and rose quickly in the estimation of his employers at Cowan and Dickinson. He was attractive, of average height, and had a trim figure and light brown curly hair. His application for pardon after the war describes him as "thirty-one years of age, five feet 10 in. high, grey eyes."[21] Later in life he grew somewhat stout and wore a full mustache. He enjoyed good food and good cigars. In his narrative he often notes with satisfaction the attention shown him by the young women of Knoxville and elsewhere. Indeed, some of his anecdotes seem intended primarily to demonstrate his success with the ladies. From all later accounts of him, however, he was a faithful husband and loving family man.

Life held great promise for an energetic young man in Knoxville at the end of the 1850s, and Reuben was "delighted beyond measure with Knoxville as a home." His salaried job and a private investment partnership had put him in a comfortable financial position by 1861. It was probably in that year that he left Knoxville to work, perhaps temporarily, in New York City, where he added to his growing successes.[22] Thus, it was with dismay that he watched the nation head toward a north-south division over states' rights and slavery. The results of secession were horrifying: "my brethren and kindred, my people of the South, arrayed one section against the other—the North coming down to conquer the South."

Reuben returned to Tennessee, probably in the early summer of 1861, and decided that he "could not desert my own people," by which he probably refers not only to his family and friends in Grainger County, but also to his roots in Virginia. It was in July, most likely the first week or so, that he entered Confederate military service at Morristown, Tennessee (then in Grainger County), as a first lieutenant in the Third Tennessee Infantry volunteer regiment.[23] He was twenty-seven years old.

Reuben's introduction to military life was stark: "The first night I spent in camp as a soldier was on the bloody field of Manassas, just after the first great battle of the war." The first battle of Manassas, a signal victory for the Confederacy, was fought on July 21, which means he probably had little or no training before being deployed. Training for volunteers in any case was sometimes brief and superficial, but he and his fellow East Tennesseans had certain advantages over urban recruits. As one contemporary diarist noted, "Our country boys have been brought up on horseback, and hunting has ever been their holiday sport."[24]

Reuben fought in several skirmishes near Washington, D.C., then went back to Tennessee to form what became Company I of the Fifty-ninth Tennessee Infantry regiment, later mounted infantry, made up of men and boys from Grainger and Hawkins Counties, which remained his outfit for the duration of the war. A recent study has shown that in such Tennessee companies the "typical enlistee was a nonslaveholding man in his early twenties, born in a small log cabin, with limited public education, who farmed for a living."[25] Company I's first commander was First Lieutenant (later Captain) William H. Smith, whom Clark replaced by late 1862 or early 1863 when Smith became ill. Clark was promoted to captain on October 17, 1863, after Smith's resignation from the service.[26] Reuben Clark saw action during the Vicksburg campaign, was an eyewitness to several important Union naval operations on the Mississippi, and endured the long siege of Vicksburg. He was taken prisoner when the Confederates surrendered Vicksburg on July 4, 1863, but, like virtually all the defenders, he was paroled and allowed to return home. After his unit was reassembled in a new command, he fought in a number of engagements in Tennessee, and later in most of the important battles as well as in numerous engagements and skirmishes of the long 1864 campaign in the Shenandoah Valley; he completed his military career in East Tennessee.

Clark's accounts of military action are uneven in their narrative detail; none even approaches the descriptiveness of a field report. There are several possible reasons for this lack of specificity. First, he says that the notes he had kept on these events did not survive. Probably more significant are the twenty-six years that had passed since hostilities ceased, years that blurred many memories of the war, enabling him to suppress those that were particularly painful. The actions for which he provides details are usually ones in which a friend of his was killed; these events he could not forget. A similar mnemonic can be found in the recollections of a Confederate chaplain in the Second Virginia Cavalry who was present at some of the same Shenandoah Valley actions as Reuben, and who wrote only of the individuals he encountered and of the awful aftermath of battles.[27] The nonchalance or swagger that sometimes characterizes Clark's accounts may well reflect his way of dealing with sickening realities he could not bring himself to describe, for after the war he was known as a caring and unassuming person.

Despite his frequent inattention to particulars, Clark nevertheless supplies useful and heretofore unknown facts about the Fifty-ninth Tennessee Regiment, the brigades in which it fought, and in a few cases, about specific battles. His most interesting contribution may be locating the regiment in Brigadier General John C. Vaughn's brigade at the battle of Piedmont on June 5, 1864, and in describing the somewhat inexplicable movement of the Fifty-ninth early in the battle. This account appears to shed light on an otherwise unexplained and disastrous error attributed to General William E. Jones, who was in overall command. In addition, Reuben may be the first to identify one of the units occupying the hills overlooking Washington in the late summer of 1861. He also reveals that the Fifty-ninth Tennessee took part in Lieutenant General Jubal A. Early's famous raid on Washington in July 1864, and in almost all the Shenandoah Valley campaign under Early in the late summer and fall of that year. Clark began his army career at Morristown, and here it ended when he was captured for the second time in a battle on October 28, 1864. As a prisoner, he was to come as close to death as he ever had on the battlefield.

William Gannaway ("Parson") Brownlow (fig. 3), a Methodist preacher, fanatical Unionist, and editor of *The Knoxville Whig and Rebel Ventilator,* reported Clark's capture with a wild-eyed accusation that Clark had murdered a Union officer. The "Parson" called for his court martial and swift execution for the alleged crime. Clark notes

Fig. 3. William G. "Parson" Brownlow. From W. G. Brownlow, *Sketches of the Rise, Progress and Decline of Secession*, frontis.

that Brownlow also accused him of killing some Union men in Virginia.[28] The Knoxville editor was so rabidly anti-Rebel that he would probably have printed his charges in any case, but on September 18, 1863, the Union provost-marshal of Knoxville, Brigadier General Samuel P. Carter, while ordering penalties for people taking the law into their own hands, urged any citizen with a legitimate complaint against a Rebel to inform the provost-marshal's office. A week later he added that anyone knowing of murder or other such crimes done by Rebels should bring their information to his attention so that the guilty could be punished.[29] Such statements were an open invitation to Brownlow to print any rumor or libel he wished against Confederates, whom he considered traitors, robbers, brigands, and criminals, all deserving of a speedy death. In Reuben's case there was an added goad to Brownlow's anger, for the young officer belonged to the military company that kept the editor under house arrest before his exile during the period of Confederate control of Knoxville (see Appendix). Another source of irritation may have been that Clark, whom Brownlow seems to have known before the war, was a Presbyterian, and the "Parson" hated Presbyterians.[30] Brownlow returned to Knoxville when Union authority was re-established there in September 1863, and from that point into the post-war era he filled his newspaper with vindictive and often incendiary accounts of actual or supposed activities of Confederates. As in the Clark affair, much of what Brownlow printed was either fictitious or so charged with vitriol as to strain credibility. The facts in Clark's case are that the Union officer was murdered, but Clark had nothing to do with the crime; and that he had never been in the town where the second killings occurred. Nevertheless, Reuben Clark suffered greatly, and almost fatally, as a result of Brownlow's machinations.[31]

With other Confederate prisoners, Clark was taken to the Knoxville County Jail (fig. 4), and there he was placed in an iron cage, an especially intriguing detail of his story. Fortunately, his brief account of the cage can be supplemented with a description by Jacob Austin Sperry, a fellow prisoner and East Tennessean:

> The upper story, where I found myself this morning, consists of three apartments—a large one on the west side, extending the whole length of the building, containing three massive iron cages about eight feet square, leaving passage ways around and between them of three or four feet. In front, bisected by the stairway, are two smaller apartments, each containing a similar cage. The filthiness of these rooms and their general forbidding aspect is indescribable.

Fig. 4. Knoxville County Jail in 1866. From Benson J. Lossing, *Pictorial History of the Civil War* 2: 38.

The din and confusion among the crowd of human beings which began at early dawn allowed me but little opportunity for reflection. By reconnoitering in and around the cages, I found that a number of paroled officers were inmates with us, they having been assigned to the cages as the most comfortable lodging places. Among them were Lieutenants Ramsey, McClung, Haines and Odell; Fred. Montgomery, telegraph operator from Bristol and Major Goforth, Superintendent of the E.T. & Va. Railroad. In the adjoining room the cage was tenanted by Col. Dick Morgan, Capt. Reuben Clark, and Capt. John Reynolds. . . . the two latter had been domesticated here some two months [Sperry arrived Dec. 22, 1864], sentenced to death by a military commission, which sentence they were deterred from executing by fear of Confederate retaliation.[32] The remaining room and its cage were occupied by Union malefactors.[33]

It is not clear if the cages in the small rooms were considered as "choice" an accommodation as those holding the paroled officers. One of the cages is pictured in Brownlow's colorful and polemical account of the Confederate period in East Tennessee (fig. 5). The scene depicted is a heart-rending one of loyalist W. H. Harrison Self, condemned by the Confederates to die for bridge burning, bidding farewell to his tearful daughter.[34] A New Yorker, Benson J. Lossing, visited and sketched the County Jail in 1866 and noted in the upper story "two [sic] immense iron cages, into which the worse criminals are put . . . [a] loathsome place" where a number of loyalists were confined during the Confederate period in Knoxville.[35]

Reuben's cage is mentioned also in letters from Robert Ould, Confederate Agent of Exchange in Richmond, to Lieutenant Colonel John E. Mulford, Federal Assistant Agent of Exchange, requesting the exchange of both Captain Clark and Captain Reynolds.[36] One letter, dated January 25, 1865, reads:

> Sir. Since the date of my letter of the 18th instant, containing a list of Confederate prisoners held in close confinement in irons, I have been reliably informed that Capt. R. G. Clarke [sic], of the Confederate Army, is now confined in an iron cage in the Knoxville jail. I have seen a letter from him. I hope you will take immediate steps for his early delivery.

The Clark letter noted by Ould has not been found. Ould wrote a more impatient letter on Feb. 25, 1865:

> Sir. Capt. R. G. Clarke, Fifty-ninth Tennessee, was a short time since confined in a cage in Knoxville jail. I will thank you to inform me why he is not treated as a prisoner of war. Will you not release him under the recent agreement?[37]

Two letters from Ould to Mulford, dated October 7 and November 8, 1864, request the release of Captain Reynolds who "is closely confined in an iron cage, eight feet square."[38] On November 8 he noted

Fig. 5. An iron cage in the Knoxville Jail, showing W. H. H. Self, a Unionist bridge-burner, bidding good-bye to his daughter. From W. G. Brownlow, *Sketches of the Rise, Progress and Decline of Secession*. opp. 321.

that Reynolds was allowed out of the cage during the day, which does not seem to have been permitted in Reuben's case. In great frustration, Ould wrote on March 13, 1865, to General Vaughn, now the Fifty-ninth Tennessee's departmental commander, explaining that all Federal prisoners whose condition permitted them to be transported had been exchanged, including "men who were charged as deserters, spies, and murderers." Thus, he concluded, if "the Federal authorities are honest in the within offer [to exchange prisoners], why will they not immediately send Captains Clarke and Reynolds?" An endorsement from Vaughn requests an exchange of a Captain Bowers for Captain Clark.[39] None of these efforts bore fruit, and Reuben was to remain a prisoner to the end of the war and beyond.

As Clark records the battles and events of his military life and describes his subsequent imprisonment, he reveals a good bit about himself both as a soldier and as a human being. Although fear must be the most fundamental emotion in warfare, Clark rarely mentions it. In fact, he may have learned to ignore it, for he recalls several occasions on which he had to be reminded by someone else that danger was near. Fearlessness engendered by fighting is not uncommon; as one Union soldier commented, "I had lost most of the horror [of those dying around him] from the intense excitement of the battle."[40] Clark was almost contemptuous of danger even after the war when, following his release from prison, he was determined to walk the streets of Knoxville despite threats against his life. At times this youthful hubris served him well. Readers will undoubtedly admire the resourceful subterfuge by which he ingratiated himself to a Union officer at the moment of his capture at Morristown. On the other hand, the poignant episode with Enoch Beeler the evening before a skirmish shows that Reuben Clark was touched by the vulnerability of others. He appears to have had a good relationship with the men he commanded, and when he mentions one of them he always has something complimentary to say. Comments about Clark later in life, when he was a successful businessman in Rome, Georgia, reinforce the picture of a kindly, likable man with great energy and considerable ability.

Although the memoir was not written until 1891, even that long after the fact Clark's analyses of the battles in which he fought can be perceptive. In the main his comments are based on his firsthand knowledge; sometimes, however, it is clear that he has done background reading to put his own experiences into context.[41] Yet there are also details that he had forgotten, confused, or conflated over the years, as seen in the memoir. His assessments of commanders on both sides are usually on the mark. As an example, he states that it was "good generalship" for the Union commander at Vicksburg, Ulysses S. Grant, to permit his soldiers to offer food immediately to the Southern troops at the surrender of the city. Clark could see that the contrast between the "bountifully supplied" Union army and the starving Confederates disaffected many of the already demoralized Southern soldiers. He notes that many of these soldiers deserted upon parole, a fact confirmed by the Compiled Service Records of his regiment. When he judges a general's strategy in a particular battle, he usually has a persuasive reason for his views.

In addition to being a lively tale that anyone can enjoy, Reuben Clark's memoir is a rare example of a Civil War narrative by an East Tennessee Confederate. Thus, it is presented here not only for its own sake, but also for the specialist looking to enrich the story of the war and its immediate aftermath with facts and comments offered by a participant in some of the events. Clark had three separately typed copies made of his text, one each for the two daughters of his first marriage and one probably for himself. Two of the copies survive, one now owned by the editor, the other by Josephine Battey Hollingsworth; the third burned many years ago in a house fire.[42] The dedication appears only in the Hollingsworth copy, suggesting that the editor's copy was Reuben's own. There is no record of a manuscript, which means he either dictated the text or destroyed the manuscript after the copies were typed. His account is given here as it appears in the two virtually identical surviving copies, retaining original spellings and punctuation. It is uncertain if the orthography is Clark's own or that of his typist. A handwritten, formal letter of 1888 suggests, however, that despite his lack of schooling he wrote and spelled English for the most part correctly, although in the memoir his spelling of names is often faulty. Editorial comments and corrections are enclosed in brackets and italicized.

The Civil War Experience of Captain Reuben G. Clark

Dedicated to my dear daughters, Rosalie and Carrie Clark. This little story of my war experience may be interesting to you in years to come and possibly to others whom you may represent; but beyond this I do not aspire to making it entertaining.

Chapter 1

First, it may be proper for me to say something of my early life previous to the war.

I was born in a log house in Grainger County, Tennessee, on the tenth day of November, 1833; and here, in this obscure home among the mountains, my childhood and boyhood days were spent, until I was sixteen years of age. My good mother, Martha Clark, now in her eightieth year, is still residing in the same house, and no amount of persuasion on the part of her children can induce her to leave it.

I started to school when eight years of age in an old field school house on my father's plantation; and for the offense of following a small boy out and forcibly taking the [restroom?] pass away from him, received a whipping the first day. This introduction to school life threw a damper upon my enthusiasm, and I concluded that going to school was not such a luxury after all. My father required my services on the farm during spring and summer, and sent me to the old field school in the winter. I may say here that as a rule the teachers could not parse "John's knife."

When sixteen years of age, with the approval of my parents I left home on foot with two dollars and a half in my pocket, for which I had sold a pig, to accept a situation with my eldest brother, who had a little store in the small town of Rutledge [Tennessee], receiving for my first year's services my board and thirty nine dollars worth of clothing. My brother, after one year, moved away to Springfield, Mo., and I went to live with Mr. Samuel Gill at Bean Station [Tennessee], near Tate Springs.[1]

After living with Mr. Gill one year, having saved most of my small salary, I concluded to spend what balance I had in an effort to obtain more education. I packed up and went back to the same little county town of Rutledge, where an Irishman, who had graduated at Dublin, Ireland, had opened school. He was finely educated and of him much was expected, but he proved to be an educated fool. All parties interested became disgusted, and his school broke down after a few weeks. This ended my efforts to obtain a school education.

My friend, Mr. Gill, then obtained for me a situation as salesman with Cowan & Dickinson, wholesale drygoods, in Knoxville, Tenn., which at that time was the largest house of the kind in the State [fig. 2].[2] I may add here that Mr. Gill always remained a true friend, and rendered me great service during the most trying days of my life.[3] He was always loyal to his friends.

Knoxville was to me a wonderful town, and the business of Cowan & Dickinson a very large one. In my efforts to satisfactorily discharge the duties assigned me, I was for a time greatly embarrassed by reason of inexperience and want of general knowledge. I had demanded the salary of an experienced salesman, and was expected to earn it. Fortunately, by close application and very hard work, I soon gained a general knowledge of the business and the customers, so that after six months of painful experience and trying discouragements it was extremely gratifying to realize that my employers regarded me with favor, and extended that courtesy which is usually accorded an employee who is faithful and whose services are counted valuable. At the expiration of the first year I was promoted from the retail to the wholesale department, and in the matter of salary and rank, had the satisfaction of knowing that I outranked gentlemen who had been in the house ten years or more.

Delighted beyond measure with Knoxville as a home, I was particularly anxious to grow in favor with my employers and to deserve the good will and encouragement of the best class of people, among whom my lot had been cast, and had the satisfaction of knowing that I succeeded in both. The world was very bright to me, and on one occasion I said to my mother that I was as happy a boy as lived on earth; to which she replied, "Yes, you always seem very happy, but I am afraid you will have trouble yet."

We shall see if it came.

Chapter 2

The Presidential contest of 1860 was approaching. The country was in a fever of excitement. "Slavery" had been the staple of congressional debate for many years, until the North and the South seemed to be gradually pulling apart. For the first time in the history of the country a strong man was nominated for president who represented a party based on opposition to slavery—Abraham Lincoln.

In the political convention of that year, John Bell, of Tennessee, was nominated by the Whig party [*or rather, the Unionist branch of the Democratic party*]; John C. Breckinridge, of Kentucky, by the [*Southern wing of the*] Democratic party, and Abraham Lincoln, of Illinois, by the Republicans.[1] The latter had no representatives in the south at that time, and was elected by northern votes. This greatly exasperated the extremists of the southern states, and greatly pleased the same class at the north. This class, on both sides, had kept up the strife, and their golden opportunity for precipitating a crisis on the country had come. One held the perpetuation of the Union as subordinate to the destruction of slavery; the other, then known as "Southern Fire-eaters," was anxious for the conflict, as was evidenced by documentary proofs, in which plans were discussed for firing up the southern heart and precipitating the southern states into a dissolution.

The Presidential contest was the most exciting ever known in the history of the country, and as it began to dawn upon the people of the south that Mr. Lincoln was going to be elected, the grave question presented itself: "What is going to be the outcome?" The Whig speakers and party were in favor of submitting, in case of his election; but the Democratic speakers would not so commit themselves.

As had been predicted, Lincoln was elected by northern votes, and South Carolina declared herself out of the Union. I belonged to the old line Whig party and was greatly exasperated at this action on the part of that State, as no overt act had been committed to provoke it—so much so that in the excitement of the moment I expressed the wish that Anderson,[2] at Fort Sumpter [sic], would blow Charleston off the ground.

Other southern states, one after the other, followed South Carolina. In the meantime the Conservatives in Congress were using every possible effort to effect a compromise by which the calamity of war might be averted, Stephen A. Douglass[3] being among the last to give it up. Mr. Douglass was a very able man, and was an Independent candidate for President in this same contest. He was United States senator from Illinois, having defeated Abraham Lincoln before the people for that office.

General Beauregard[4] was massing troops at Charleston in front of Fort Sumpter. The Fort was being reinforced by the Federals, and at this juncture Gen. Beauregard fired on the U.S. flag, compelling Maj. Anderson's surrender.

The effect was electrifying, both north and south. The war was on! [*RGC was in New York at the time.*] The whole north was in a white heat of excitement. President Lincoln issued a proclamation calling for seventy five thousand troops to suppress the rebellion, and volunteers were pouring into Washington from every northern state.

There was a corresponding uprising in the south. The martial spirit was fired up, and patriotic impulse throbbed in every bosom. Thus ended all effort of diplomacy to avert the impending calamity, and war with all its horrors confronted us. Whatever might have been our opinions as to the abstract right of secession and inadequate cause for war, the reality was upon us. Jefferson Davis[5] had been elected President of the Confederate States, and with his Cabinet and counsellors, was moving with all the power at his command for the defense of the south. The situation was one to which the south's grandest statesman, John C. Calhoun,[6] had pointed with a prophet's finger long years before.

There was no alternative but to take sides in this bloody conflict. What should I do? I had opposed secession and did not regard the election of Abraham Lincoln as just cause for war. Here were my brethren and kindred, my people of the South, arrayed one section against the other—the North coming down to conquer the South.

I could not desert my own people, and so entered the Confederate army in July, 1861 [*as a first lieutenant in the Third Tennessee Regiment, commanded by then Colonel John C. Vaughn of Tennessee,*[7] *in the Fourth Brigade under Brigadier General Arnold Elzey in General Joseph E. Johnston's division, Confederate Army of the Shenandoah*],[8] in which army I fought until captured the second time at Morristown in the winter of 1864–1865. [*Vaughn, promoted to brigadier in September 1862, would be his commander through much of the war.*]

Chapter 3

The first night I spent in camp as a soldier was on the bloody field of Manassas [Virginia], just after the first great battle of the war, which was fought July 21st, 1861. [*This is the first battle of Manassas, or Bull Run, Virginia, won decisively by the Confederates. The regiment had left Knoxville June 2, 1861 and arrived and encamped at Winchester, Virginia, on June 24.*[1]] The dead and dying were all around us, and prisoners were being brought in and disposed of. This seemed to me a fearful introduction to the realities of war, and I laid down in camp that night sadly impressed with the fact that, notwithstanding our great victory, we had undertaken a serious job. Many of my young friends had fallen in this battle, and we sat down to talk about them, discussing their good qualities, sympathizing with their kindred and bemoaning their loss. It did seem sad that these brave young men should have to fall in this first engagement. What desolation was wrought in the homes from which they had but recently gone out!

We rested for the night, and next morning moved on to Fairfax Station [Virginia]. The brigade taking the advance, and commanded by General Elsey,[2] of Baltimore, was composed of the First Maryland, Third Tennessee, Eleventh and Thirteenth Virginia regiments—the latter commanded by Col. A. P. Hill, who was afterwards made Lieut. General.[3]

General Elsey had his headquarters in a small church, whose steeple can still be seen from the train approaching Washington from Lynchburg [Virginia]. There was another church at this point, a very old structure, with seats boxed in with room for eight people to sit facing each other. This church was built by Mr. Fairfax, an English gentleman, who was a close friend to General Washington up to the Revolutionary War.[4] Mr. Fairfax remained loyal to the British government, and upon that question they separated.

After camping at this point a few days, we were ordered forward to take possession of Munson's Hill [Virginia], a high point in full view of the capitol at Washington, and at this point I had my first experience in fighting Yankees [fig. 6]. [*From September 6 to 12 and 22 to 26 the regiment is recorded as being on "Grand Guard" at Munson's Hill.*][5] On the evening of our arrival we had thrown up temporary breastworks on the hill, and late in the day the Yankees moved out of the woods and opened fire upon us, but were driven back. The great victory at Manassas had broken the spirit of the northern troops for a time, and there was little to relieve the monotony of camp life, except occasional skirmishing with the Yankee outposts. [*The dispirited state of Union troops was not the only reason for the extended lull in fighting. Soon after Manassas, voices in the South asked why the Confederate generals did not pursue the advantage of their victory, and march forthwith on Washington. Many reasons were given—disorganized or green troops, insufficient supplies and rations, adverse weather conditions—but clear explanations were not forthcoming then, nor are they now.*][6] I obtained permission [in late September 1861] to return home and make up a company, and having succeeded, went [about February 17, 1862] into Col. Burch Cook's[7] 59th Tennessee regiment [*actually the First Battalion of Tennessee Infantry under Major William L. Eakin; the Fifty-ninth Tennessee was not formed until May 1862; see Appendix*] at Morristown, Tenn., under Gen. E. Kirby Smith,[8] who was then commanding the department of East Tennessee, with headquarters at Knoxville. [*At the time, RGC's rank was still first lieutenant. During the winter of 1861 the First Battalion was encamped at Knoxville for training and for guard duty in the city and on passenger trains.*[9] *In June 1862, the newly formed Fifty-ninth Tennessee regiment was sent to Strawberry Plains, Tennessee, to guard against Union saboteurs.*[10] *The regiment appears on a July 3 list with the Fifth Brigade of Brigadier General Carter L. Stevenson's division.*[11] *By July 21, 1862, RGC was in Knoxville, for an unspecified time, where he signed for the purchase of a canteen.*[12] *His company was ordered to Noes Ferry, Tennessee, in September 1862, and stayed there until October 16.*[13]] Upon the return of

CHAPTER 3

Fig. 6. Munson's Hill, Virginia. From Johnson and Buel, eds., *Battles and Leaders of the Civil War* 2: 115.

Gen. Bragg's[14] army [about October 10, 1862] from Kentucky after a brief and unsuccessful campaign [*culminating in the indecisive Confederate defeat at Perryville on October 8,*[15] *on October 16 at Tazewell, Tennessee, Company I rejoined its regiment, which was now encamped for the winter at Lenoir, Tennessee.*[16] *About December 18 or shortly after*], my regiment was ordered to Vicksburg, Miss. [*with Stevenson's division*].[17] We were stopped at Dalton, Ga., to wait for supplies to come up,[18] and whilst there, received intelligence of the death of Maj. Charles M. Alexander, whom we had left in Knoxville sick.[19] Maj. Alexander was a special friend of mine, and a very handsome and accomplished young man, immensely popular, and although quite young, had been elected to one of the highest offices in the State. When the war broke out, he joined my company as a private, and was elected Major of the regiment at its organization.[20] He left a wife and one child. His wife's maiden name was Miss Lucy Cowan,[21] than whom one more lovable never blessed the household of any man.

[*Vicksburg, Mississippi, high on a bluff overlooking the great waterway dividing the East and the Midwest, was considered by both sides to be an essential gateway to the Confederate south and to be well nigh impregnable.*

By the spring of 1862 the Mississippi was a major priority on the Union list of targets for assault, and for Vicksburg that meant attacks by both land and water. When New Orleans fell to a U.S. naval squadron under then Captain David G. Farragut on April 25, that left Vicksburg "the most important strategic position in the Confederacy."[22] Since spring, reinforcements had been arriving in Vicksburg from many regions of the South, including Tennessee.]

Our journey to Vicksburg was a succession of ovations all the way. The approaching enemy from the west excited the people, who were now thoroughly aroused. We were greeted all along the way with cheers, smiles, bouquets and good things generally. [*Such accolades from the local populace, especially from women, were common in the early days of the war.*] We arrived in Vicksburg in one of the stormiest nights I have ever experienced, and had orders to proceed immediately to the battlefield, where Gen. McClerndon[23] had attacked Gen. Smith[24] that afternoon [*in the battle of Chickasaw Bluff, December 29, 1862*].[25] We were compelled to march quite a distance through the swamps and thickets, and having no guide furnished us, it was impossible to make our way through the thick darkness in the midst of the terrible rain storm until daylight, so it was sunrise before we arrived at the point designated. [*Commander David Dixon Porter,[26] a key Union commander in the river battle for Vicksburg, wrote that the "level lands were inundated, and there were three feet of water in the swamps. . . ."*][27] For this noncompliance with Gen. Stephenson's[28] orders, Col. Cook, who commanded our regiment, was arrested and ordered to be tried by Court Martial— a humiliation which he felt very keenly, for he was a proud man. [*The trial was held and Cooke was acquitted.*][29] Lieut. Col. Aikin[30] here took command of the regiment, but the battle was over. McClerndon, in command of the Yankee forces, had been repulsed, and under cover of darkness returned to his gunboats from which he had landed, and moved up to Arkansas Post [Arkansas], where he captured our forces at that point after a bloody battle [January 10–11, 1863.]

[*On October 31, 1862, the regiment had been listed as an unattached unit in the Fourth Brigade of Colonel Alexander W. Reynolds[31] (fig. 7); by January 31, 1862, the Fifty-ninth Tennessee had been made part of the Fourth Brigade.*][32]

Fig. 7. Colonel (later Brigadier General) Alexander W. Reynolds. Photograph courtesy of the U.S. Army Military History Institute, Carlisle, Pennsylvania.

(Soon after the war was over, I happened to be passing up the Arkansas River and the boat stopped at Arkansas Post, where some one called my attention to the boots of the Yankee dead sticking out at the river bank, exposed by the continual washing away of the dirt. It is to be hoped the remains of these poor, dead soldiers have been removed and given a decent burial.) [*These were almost certainly Confederate dead, who were hastily buried in their rifle pits and trenches just after the Union victory at Arkansas Post, January 11, 1863, with no further disposition of the bodies. The rifle pits extended from Post Bayou, away from the river, to the fort on the river.*][33]

Vicksburg is on the left side of the Mississippi, about four hundred miles above New Orleans, population in 1860, 5,000. The capture of New Orleans in 1862 [April 25] gave the Federals virtual possession of the Mississippi to this point, down to which operations from above had cleared the way to the Federals. In May [18], 1862, a portion of Farragut's[34] fleet, under Captain Lee,[35] appeared on the opposite side of Vicksburg and demanded the surrender of the city on pain of bombardment. This was promptly refused, but no bombardment ensued. On June 28th Farragut again attempted a bombardment, but decided that Vicksburg could not be taken without a stronger force, and when the river began falling he was obliged to descend to New Orleans. Thus for five months there were no further operations against Vicksburg.[36]

Meanwhile, the Confederates had erected fortifications at Port Hudson [Louisiana], on a high bluff about one hundred and twenty miles below Vicksburg.[37] Our position had been strengthened all along the shores. Porter's gunboats were evidently endeavoring to run the gauntlet by our line of batteries.

Nothing had happened during the fall [1862] of any importance, except occasional skirmishes with Yankee outposts, the capture of small detachments of Federals who ventured across to our side above and below our fortifications, and the ceaseless roar of Porter's mortars as they sent their immense shells heavenward from the peninsula [*the*

CHAPTER 3

Fig. 8. Confederate Battery at Vicksburg. From *Harper's Weekly*, 1863, p. 489.

De Soto Peninsula, across from Vicksburg, formed by a sharp bend in the Mississippi River.] Many nights have I watched their course by the burning fuses as they made their circuit through the air. We were camped on the commanding heights below the city, from which the movements of Porter's fleets could be observed [fig. 8]. [*By this time RGC was company commander, replacing Captain William H. Smith, who suffered from tuberculosis.*][38] Anxious to see the long anticipated attempt by the Yankee fleet to run by Vicksburg, we were delighted to see them moving down [February 2, 1863]. The river here was over a mile wide, and as the two boats steamed down close to the farther shore, the excitement was intense. The rear boat backed out [of formation] and returned up the river before reaching our heavy artillery, but the other, which proved to be the "Queen of the West," went by, hugging the other shore, with all the speed she could command, looking almost like a black streak, with our batteries thundering upon her like an avalanche. But she went through without loss, except slight damage to her hull.[39]

At this success of Porter's attempt to put gunboats through, we were sadly disappointed and chagrinned, as we had thought it entirely impossible for the enemy to pass our heavy artillery. The light Confederate gunboat ["Desoto"] up Red River must now either capture this "Queen of the West" or be captured by her; so selecting its men for the attack, it steamed out of Red River and up the Mississippi in the night [February 14, 1863] until it came in sight, and having all on board in readiness, with all the force they could command, made toward the "Queen" with the hope to sink her by running into her. [*The "Queen" had already been fired upon by shore batteries and had run aground.*] The first charge failed to accomplish this, and as our boat drew back to charge again, one of the heavy guns of the "Queen" came very near disabling her, but with the courage that knows no fear the little crew, in a second charge, disabled the "Queen," captured her crew and took them on board prisoners. Both boats were promptly sent up Red River for repairs. [*RGC was not an eyewitness to these events, which took place in the Red River, not the Mississippi.*][40]

Just at this time [March 25, 1863] the flag ship, "Hartford" [fig. 9], with fifty two guns, steamed up in sight of our pickets at Warrenton [Mississippi].[41] Warrenton was six miles below Vicksburg, and we were down in the flat near the river in a small dirt fort some twenty feet thick, covered with railroad iron, expecting to be attacked by this boat at any hour. I well remember standing out on top as she moved up with her dark cloud of smoke. The first shell came whizzing by [about 7:15 A.M.], which was a signal for every fellow to get to his post, both for self-protection and to be ready to fire on the enemy in case he attempted to land. The boat came up close to the front [?fort] and began turning round in the river and firing so rapidly that it was impossible to count the number of shots. [*The "Hartford's" fire power was augmented by the gunboat "Albatross," which had been lashed to the flagship slightly abaft on her port side.*][42] In fact, we were almost buried with the dirt thrown on us by the guns of the boat, so terrific was the firing. In conjunction with this movement, Porter had started some more iron-clads [toward Vicksburg] from above—this time with far less success than before.[43] One of these boats [the ram "Switzerland"] was sinking and gave the alarm of distress, which caused the

CHAPTER 3

Fig. 9. U.S.S. *Hartford*, flagship of Admiral David G. Farragut. From Benson J. Lossing, *Pictorial History of the Civil War* 2: 335.

"Hartford" to go to the rescue of the sinking vessel [*which did not sink but managed to float downstream out of danger*], and we got on the fort just in time to see the second Yankee boat [the ram "Lancaster"] go down, leaving her smokestack in sight and her men struggling in the water for the shore [fig. 10]. The booming of cannons and shouting of men seemed almost to shake the ground, so tremendous was the noise. And we greatly enjoyed the victory.

Gen. Grant[44] then began cutting a canal across the peninsula in order to get his fleet and army to a point below Vicksburg, where he could cross his troops and surround us. [*Rising and falling water levels made passage of supplies through the canal impractical. In the meantime, with the aid of Admiral Porter's ironclad gunboats, Grant managed to run a supply fleet by Vicksburg itself on April 16, while his troops moved down the west bank of the river.*][45] It was on the 29th of April, 1863, that he succeeded in landing a division near Port Gibson [at Bruinsburg, Mississippi],

Fig. 10. U.S.S. *Switzerland* and U.S.S. *Lancaster* under Confederate fire at Vicksburg. From *Harper's Weekly*, 1863, p. 241.

some thirty miles below.[46] I was on picket duty at Warrenton when orders came to report with my men to my commander [Colonel Reynolds] without delay. We were put on a forced march to Port Gibson without even time to prepare rations, and arrived there, fatigued and hungry, at ten o'clock that night. Gen. Tillman [read Tracy][47] had met the advance of Gen. Grant's forces and engaged them in battle [May 1, 1863]. The fight was kept up until dark, when Gen. Tillman [i.e., Tracy] fell mortally wounded and died a few moments afterward [*Tilghman was killed soon after at the battle of Champion Hill*]. Worn out with fatigue and hunger, we laid down in hearing of the enemy; but our rest was of short duration, as we were called up at two o'clock in the morning and ordered back in the direction of Vicksburg in order to avoid being cut off by a flank movement of the enemy. We then fell back across Big Black River and camped in a large magnolia grove for several days. In the meantime, Gen. Grant had marched with his army in the direction of Jackson, Miss., and turned back on Vicksburg with his entire army of sixty six thousand men. It was now evident that the supreme hour of trial had come. Our army of thirty thousand men had been starved out and reduced by sickness until we had only sixteen thousand discouraged soldiers with which to confront the overwhelming forces under Gen. Grant. Gen. Pemberton, the commander of our forces, was regarded a very weak man and wholly incompetent for his position, but he was a personal favorite of President Davis.[48] On the morning of the 16th of May the battle [*of Champion Hill or Baker's Creek*] for the possession of the Mississippi Valley occurred.[49] Just before it began, my Colonel handed me an appeal in circular form from the General in command to be read to my company, then the largest in the brigade. [*This probably refers to the emotional call to arms written by Pemberton four days earlier.*][50] This was a dark, gloomy morning, and as I ordered my men in line under the trees to read to them the address, the expression of their faces so impressed me that I can never forget the events of that morning. We fully realized that we had inadequate numbers and an incompetent general [?Pemberton], and our chances for victory were hopeless—that a fruitless sacrifice of life was to be made that day.

The battle opened about nine o'clock, and before noon we discovered that Grant's lines were being thrown in our rear; his lines being so much longer than ours, we were forced to retreat across the [Big Black] river, back in the direction of Vicksburg.[51] Why General Pemberton left the high commanding points on the Vicksburg side of the river and crossed to the low flat to meet Grant, leaving the heights [of the Vicksburg area] and the [Mississippi] river behind him, has always been a mystery to me. [*In fact, Pemberton had wanted to concentrate on defending Vicksburg, and the decision to advance was arrived at after much wrangling by his commanders, and in response to an order from his superior, General Joseph E. Johnston.*][52] From Big Black River we fell back across the ravine, leaving many killed and wounded.[53] Gen. Lowring,[54] in command of the division on the right of our army, had the sagacity to see the utter hopelessness of trying to defend Vicksburg under General Pemberton, and not being covered by the enemy, availed himself of the opportunity to move out and escape with one of the best divisions of the army. [*Loring's escape was largely accidental. General Tilghman's brigade protected the Confederate route of retreat, the endeavor in which Tilghman was killed.*[55] *Colonel Reynolds's brigade had been deployed as the rear guard, in charge of protecting the supply trains, for which duty he and his officers received praise from both Pemberton and Carter Stevenson. Retreating back toward Vicksburg, the brigade encountered heavy shelling as well as fighting, in an action known at the battle of the Big Black River. Reynolds saved many of his troops from Union guns or capture by taking a roundabout, cross-country trek to reach his command as it fell back toward the city.*][56]

Chapter 4

[*On its return to Vicksburg the Fifty-ninth Tennessee was assigned to the trenches on the far right, south of Vicksburg.*][1] Gen. Grant invested Vicksburg on the 18th of May, and stormed our fortifications on the 19th. This effort to carry our position by storm was disastrous to the Federals. Their battle lines, one after the other, emerged from the woods, coming across the old field in our front three lines deep, when all but the front line gave way under our deadly fire, leaving the front unsupported. This line, however, be it said to their credit, moved right up under the galling fire of shot and shell from our fortifications until they came just in front of our entrenchments, where, upon reaching and finding themselves unsupported, they had no alternative but to surrender.[2] The killed of the Federals in this charge were left in front of our entrenchments until decomposition set in and they became very offensive. Gen. Pemberton sent a flag of truce to ask Gen. Grant if he was not going to bury his dead, and if not, to suspend hostilities until we could bury them ourselves. In response to this message a detail of men was sent over from the Federal army, and holes were dug and the Yankee dead were shovelled into them without removing cartridge boxes or any of their equipment. Whether it was General Grant's intention to leave his dead near our line to make it so disagreeable that we could not endure the stench, or what his purpose was in neglecting to put away his dead soldiers, I have never understood. [*Another eyewitness reported that the dead were left not on the 19th, but after* the July 22d assault, and that there were also wounded "suffering fearful agonies." He noted that the truce lasted two and one-half hours, and both sides buried the dead and aided the wounded.]³ With this experiment, Gen. Grant decided never to make another charge upon our fortifications, but began preparations for a long siege, which finally resulted in the surrender of thirty thousand Confederates on the 4th day of July, 1863.

Grant's loss at Vicksburg, as officially reported, was eight thousand, five hundred and seventy five men. The Confederates lost about ten thousand. The hardships and deprivations of our men during that siege were beyond description. Our source of supplies had been cut off long before the siege of Vicksburg, and we had been for months living on beef from cattle that were so poor they could not get up off the ground when down, and before the siege ended, our soldiers were only too glad to get mule meat. [*On July 1, 1863, Colonel A. W. Reynolds wrote to General Stevenson, the division commander, that his troops were "much reduced in strength, and in many instances entirely prostrated," many in the hospital.*⁴ *On June 28, 1863, Pemberton received a letter, signed "Many Soldiers" and begging for food: "Our rations have been cut down to one biscuit and a small bit of bacon per day. . . . If you can't feed us, you had better surrender us. . . . This army is now ripe for mutiny, unless it can be fed."*⁵] The siege lasted forty seven days—days of dreadful suspense, privation and peril.⁶

For a short time our picket lines were kept in front of the entrenchments, but they were finally driven back to the breastworks. The Federal forces dug roads up near our lines, and then parallelled them deep enough to run four-horse teams at close range in perfect safety. In fact, they worked themselves up so close that it was worth one's life to put his head above the breastworks for any length of time. The ground between the two armies was covered with thickets of bushes, briers, etc., and pickets were placed in front at night to avoid surprise. On one occasion when I was Field Officer of the Day, visiting the different posts, I had passed my men and was nearing the Yankee posts, which would have cost me my life within a moment's time had I not heard a gentle whistle of warning; the posts were so close to each other that we dared not make any noise, and it being dark, I failed to see my men. It was the duty of the Field Officer to visit each picket post in front of the brigade during the night, watching every movement of the enemy, and report next morning at headquarters.

There were a great many casualties during the siege. I can not tell how many men I saw killed in various ways; some torn to pieces by accidental shells, others shot in the head by sharp shooters, etc., etc. I commanded two companies [*the second unidentified*] in support of a Maryland battery, in charge of Captain Clairborne,[7] who was shot almost to pieces in an artillery duel three weeks after the siege began. I was standing by, looking at him, forgetful of my danger, when some one cried out, "Get out of the way, Clark, you will be killed!" The greatest mortality in our army during this siege—and, indeed, during the Mississippi campaign—was from sickness.[8]

Finally the end of the dreadful campaign came. It was a beautiful day on the 4th of July, 1863. We were surrendered as prisoners of war. [*As the Confederates surrendered, one Union division cheered "the gallant defenders of Vicksburg."*][9] Gen. Grant, thinking that possibly we were starved out, permitted his men to come among us with well filled haversacks which they opened up at once, asking us to help ourselves from them, saying "We know you must be hungry." This kindness had more significance than a mere friendly act; it was good generalship. The contrast was so great between their well fed and bountifully supplied army and our starved forces, that it disaffected many of our men, especially the lower classes, so that when we were exchanged it was impossible to get many of them back into the army.[10] This class had had enough of privations and suffering, and having but little pride or character, they preferred the disgrace which attached to desertion rather than continue in the service.

Chapter 5

I think it was on the 12th of July [the 10th] that we were given our paroles as prisoners of war,[1] and under a burning July sun, started through the sand bottoms of Mississippi, one hundred and sixty miles to the Mobile & Ohio railroad. Upon our arrival at Mobile [Alabama] we were greeted as the heroes of Vicksburg, and for the first time in years were free from the restraints of military rule. [*Thirty-day and ninety-day leaves were authorized for the Vicksburg parolees, the longer period for those who lived far from the Mississippi theater.*[2] *The Fifty-ninth Tennessee must have qualified for a ninety-day leave.*]

Arriving at Knoxville, Tennessee, on the 15th of July [by railroad] I greatly enjoyed the hospitality of my old friends. Also visited Mont Vale Springs [Tennessee], where I made a great many pleasant acquaintances. It was indeed a delightful experience, both of social pleasures and the good things of this world. This soon came to an end, however, as Gen. Buckner,[3] then in command of the Confederate forces at Knoxville, found it necessary to evacuate at the approach [the end of August] of Gen. Burnsides.[4] I remained behind with friends as long as possible, and left at night to avoid again falling into the hands of Federals, and joined some fellow parole soldiers at Wytheville, Virginia. We were exchanged in September [12th] of that year, and ordered to Decatur, Georgia,[5] and upon arrival at that point were ordered to join Gen. Joseph E. Johnston's[6] army at Dalton, Georgia,

CHAPTER 5

after the battle of Chic[k]amauga, which occurred on the 19th of September, 1863.[7]

I was then ordered to take charge of Athens, Tennessee, with my company, and here for a few weeks greatly enjoyed the society of old acquaintances and friends. [*On October 17, 1863, RGC was made a captain, probably while at Dalton, where his former company commander, Captain Smith, resigned from the army on October 11; see Appendix.*] I had my quarters with the family of Mr. Thomas Cleag, then a banker of that place, who married the eldest daughter of Judge Van Dyke,[8] a very hospitable and excellent lady. I still have delightful recollections of the pleasant associations which it was my good fortune to enjoy with Miss Fannie Van Dyke[9] and her cousin, Miss Smith,[10] and others. Of the Van Dykes I shall have more to say hereafter.

[*By November 6, 1863, the Fifty-ninth Tennessee joined the brigade of Brigadier General John C. Vaughn (fig. 11), who as a colonel had commanded RGC's first regiment, the Third Tennessee Infantry.*][11]

General Thomas's[12] cavalry was moving on Athens, and I was ordered to retreat to Loudon [Tennessee], an engine and car having been sent down to carry us to that point. [*Both Athens and Loudon are located south of Knoxville on what was the East Tennessee and Georgia Railway line, linking Knoxville with Chattanooga and Atlanta.*] In getting up my men and their plunder, I was left [behind], with two of my men, the engineer being so badly frightened that he would not wait until I could get to the depot. We had to walk thirty miles, and avoid the road to keep from being captured. Arriving at Loudon, I was ordered to take my men and destroy five engines and trains by running them into the river.[13] Having an engineer furnished me, I accomplished this job just in time to join the line of battle to meet the enemy, then coming in sight [*for a skirmish near Loudon, probably on December 4, 1863*].[14] It was late, however, and but little fighting was done as the darkness closed in on us, and we withdrew, crossing the river on

Fig. 11. Brigadier General John C. Vaughn. Photograph courtesy of the Huntington Library, San Marino, California.

pontoon bridges to join Gen. Longstreet[15] at Knoxville [December 5, 1863].

The population of Knoxville at that time was about eight thousand. The forces under Burnsides, who had been driven in from Campbell's Station [Tennessee], went into Knoxville panic-stricken.[16] Then Gen. Longstreet waited until the Federals regained confidence and were well fortified, and then made the disastrous charge on Fort Saunders [Knoxville, November 29, 1863]. Why he did so has all the while been a mystery. I believe that Gen. Stonewall Jackson[17] would have captured Knoxville with Burnsides's army within three hours after his arrival in front of the Federal lines. Gen. Longstreet was a good subordinate fighter, but not a successful department commander [*a view shared by twentieth-century historians*].

We arrived at Knoxville on the 5th of December, and found Gen. Longstreet raising the siege and moving into upper Tennessee, where he went into winter quarters [at Rogersville.] The weather was intensely cold, and there was but little to relieve the monotony of camp life, except the usual skirmishings along the lines. Now and then detachments were sent out to capture the Federal outposts and get supplies. It was on one of these expeditions that we captured a portion of an Indiana regiment, together with some plundering citizens who had taken shelter under the Federal pickets. Among the number was one John Gray, who had made himself very obnoxious by cruel treatment to the families of the Confederate soldiers.[18] This man, who was called "Major Gray," was shot, and [William G.] Brownlow charged in his "Knoxville Whig and Rebel Ventilator" that I had had it done. Upon what grounds he made the charge I do not know, unless it was because my aged father and mother were among the sufferers at the hands of the marauder.[19] I was not in command of the expedition, and have never had any knowledge as to who killed Gray.

Among other charges which Mr. Brownlow brought against me was that I had had some men shot at Saltville, Virginia, after they had surrendered in the spring of 1864, when, as a matter of fact I had not been at Saltville during the war.[20]

Chapter 6

In the early summer we were ordered to report at Staunton, Virginia [*an important railroad center*], and upon the day of our arrival at the place [June 4, 1864], were ordered out to meet Gen. Hunter[1] at Piedmont, a small town a few miles out, where a bloody conflict ensued. The battle began in the morning [June 5, 1864] and was hotly contested.[2] My regiment [*which was with Vaughn on the right,*][3] was ordered to "double quick" to the left, where the enemy were throwing a heavy force and attempting to break our line. [*This action may have been about 1:30 P.M., noted by General Hunter as the time when Rebel troops were massing on their left.*[4] *The move may have resulted from Vaughn's misunderstanding of a message from the commander, Brigadier General William E. Jones.*[5] *In other words, the Fifty-ninth may have been sent by mistake to the far left, causing the infamous gap between the troops of Vaughn and Brigadier General John D. Imboden on the right, and infantry to their left.*[6] *Union forces made a number of assaults against this weak spot in Confederate defenses while a Union brigade under Brigadier General George Crook made its way under cover to a position from which it could successfully attack the Confederate right.*[7]] The Federal forces, seeing our movement, opened a deadly fire upon us as we passed up the hill, killing and wounding a large number of our men, among them three captains of the regiment and Major Hays.[8] We got into position, however, and repulsed the Federal forces three times, and as they gave way the third time I was giving orders to "charge" when I heard men crying out, "surrender, d—n you!," and looking back, saw the Federals had carried our right and were coming on us in the rear. Col. Aikin and many others were already prisoners. I jumped about fifteen feet down the river bank [*on the far left of the Confederate battle line*] and ran out under fire up the river and made my escape with a Lieut. Wilson, who had some holes shot in his clothing, but neither one of us was hurt.[9] We finally got into the old field, in company with six or eight others, who were making their way across to join our retreating forces; and when about the middle of the field I heard a yell in the rear. Looking back, I saw a company of Federal cavalry coming through the fence, and I cried "Boys, for God's sake stop and fire on those fellows!" We gave them one shot and they stopped to form, thus giving us time to reach the woods and join our commands.

Our complete surprise by the enemy may be easily accounted for. My regiment was fighting just over the brow of a hill near the Shenandoah River and the fighting was so fierce, both with artillery and musketry, that from our position it was impossible to tell which army was carrying the day. [*Jones, however, had evidently ignored a warning about Crook's movements.*[10] *After the battle the Southern press was scathing in its condemnation of Imboden and Vaughn for holding fire, despite the pleas of their men, as Crook's troops descended upon them, but both generals may have thought they had been told to await an order to fire.*[11]] Gen. Jones, the brave commander of our forces, fell from his horse, shot to death. My Colonel Aiken and eighty officers and men of the regiment were killed and captured [*Eakin was among those captured*].

We fell back to the mountains in the direction of Charlotte[sville, Virginia], where Gen. Breckenridge[12] took command next morning [June 6, 1864; fig. 12]. [*Following Jones's death, the command of his forces devolved upon Vaughn.*[13] *As the much depleted and disorganized Confederates fell back, Vaughn was able to salvage supplies and to proceed south that night through New Hope to Fishersville. The next day he set up headquarters*

Fig. 12. Major General John C. Breckinridge. Photograph courtesy of the U.S. Army Military History Institute, Carlisle, Pennsylvania.

in a railroad tunnel at Rockfish Gap in the Blue Ridge Mountains.[14] *When Breckinridge took command, RGC's regiment, along with other troops of Vaughn's brigade, mounted in December, was now dismounted.*[15]]

Gen. Hunter, after defeating us at Piedmont, made a forced march for Lynchburg [Virginia], expecting to capture that city before we could reach there or reinforcements could be sent from Richmond. [*Breckinridge, anticipating Hunter's move, led the troops of Vaughn's command from June 12 to 16 south through the mountains to Lynchburg.*[16] *RGC appears to confuse this exhausting march with the retreat to Rockfish Gap after the battle of Piedmont.*] We crossed the mountains that night just in time to get into a strong position to meet Hunter's command, and having received reinforcements from Richmond, we were well prepared to receive the enemy—a fact that he fully realized himself, as he only put out his skirmish line to open on us, whilst he moved down the valley in the direction of Salem.[17] [*In fact, the Confederates were not in*

CHAPTER 6

Fig. 13. Lieutenant General Jubal A. Early, portrait by John Wycliffe Lowes Forster. Photograph courtesy of the Virginia Historical Society, Richmond, Virginia.

that good a position. Breckinridge was still recovering from an injury incurred when his horse was shot, and his troops were exhausted and their numbers much depleted by the defeat at Piedmont. Lieutenant General Jubal A. Early[18] (fig. 13), sent by General Robert E. Lee on the virtually impossible mission of defending the Shenandoah, brought his army by a long march and finally by train to Lynchburg on June 17. With a number of aggressive moves against the Federals during that afternoon, and by running locomotives in and out of Lynchburg all night, Early tricked Hunter into believing that the Confederates would far outnumber the Union forces. Hunter withdrew before morning's light on June 18.[19]] Gen. Breckenridge followed him as far as Salem, a distance of fifty miles, when Hunter, being hard pressed, stopped to fight long enough to let his wagon teams get out of the way [June 21]. With this he succeeded, with the exception of eleven pieces of artillery and a few loads of supplies, which fell into our hands.

We followed Hunter's command along the old Valley of Virginia

Fig. 14. "Federal Troops Burning in the Shenandoah Valley," drawing by Theodore R. Davis. From S. W. Sears, ed., *Century Collection of Civil War Art*, 1974, p. 321.

[Shenandoah Valley] into Maryland. [*Confederates fought engagements with Hunter's forces at New Castle, Virginia, and Sweet Sulphur Spring and Cove Gap, West Virginia on June 23.*[20] *By now Hunter's troops were exhausted and without food stores, and the Southerners turned their attention elsewhere.*] Here Gen. Early, with reinforcements, took command and [July 9, 1864] we met the Federal Gen. Wallace[21] near Relay Station [at Monocacy], between Washington and Baltimore. After a short, sharp fight, with considerable loss on both sides, Gen. Wallace was defeated and fell back to Baltimore. [*The troops in Early's command were tired, and had suffered substantial losses in previous actions. Instead of being able to press his advantage and continue on into Washington, Early waited for two days, giving Federal forces ringing the city time to bring in reinforcements and organize their defense.*][22]

[*In the following paragraph RGC's chronology is again disordered.*] General Hunter burned houses indiscriminately along the Valley of Virginia [fig. 14],[23] and Gen. Early, to show the Federals that two could

Fig. 15. "Confederate Forces Crossing the Potomac in 1862." From *Harper's Weekly*, 1862, p. 613.

play at that game, gave orders that the women and children be moved out of Chambersburg [Pennsylvania] without delay, and burn the town in retaliation. It was a distressing scene to witness [July 30–31, 1864], and one among the many horrible expedients of war. [*Actually, Brigadier General John McCausland was ordered first to demand a large indemnity from Chambersburg for Hunter's destruction in the Valley, and if payment were denied, to torch the town. In support of McCausland, Early took Vaughn's brigade and the divisions of Major General Robert E. Rodes and Major General Stephen D. Ramseur on July 29 to Williamsport, Maryland. A mounted force from Vaughn's command then routed Federal cavalry at Williamsport and on July 30 moved on to Hagerstown, 22 miles south of Chambersburg.*[24] *It is thus unlikely that RGC saw the burning city.*] Gen. Early then [*or rather, after the battle of Monocacy*] moved on Washington [July 11–12], approaching as near with his advance guard as Fourteenth Street [*actually, as far as Fort Stevens on the Seventh Street Road*],[25] his object being to make a feint on Washington to draw the Federal troops from Richmond.[26] [*In any case, once again the condition of his troops, burdened by plunder and numerous prisoners taken along on the march to the Federal capital, and debilitated by crushing mid-summer heat, forced Early to withdraw after meeting heavy resistance from Federal defenders.*][27] We then fell back into Virginia [fig. 15] and were pursued by Gen. Hunter's army until we passed Winchester [Virginia], and halted at New Town [Virginia].[28] Here the Federal army again attacked us [*in a skirmish on July 22, 1864*], and were badly defeated.[29] I was sent forward with a detail from my regiment to meet the Federal advance in front of our brigade. The whole Yankee battle line was moving on us, and being nearly out of ammunition I sent a runner for more, and to ascertain what I must do. About this time, and just as my messenger started, I received orders to fall back into the general line. In this skirmish I lost my faithful orderly sergeant, Samuel West.[30]

The two divisions, one under Gen. Breckenridge [*including the Fifty-ninth Tennessee*] and the other under Gen. Hunter [*actually two divisions under Brigadier General George Crook*], were each making for the high grounds from which I had fallen back, and seeing that they were going to come in sight of each other at very close range, I was intensely interested, as everything now depended upon quick, sharp and bold work. [*This action is known as the second battle of Kernstown, on July 24*]. The Federals were routed in about twenty minutes, during which time the fighting was terrific.[31] We pressed the Federals through Winchester and down the valley beyond the Potomac River, capturing supply trains and provisions on the way.[32] [*Here RGC conflates almost two months of moves by Early to clear the northern Shenandoah Valley of Union forces, successful for a time, but giving way in mid-August to Major General Philip H. Sheridan's*[33] *advance into Virginia.*][34] We then went into camp at Winchester, but were able to get but little rest, as Gen. Sheridan was marching on us with heavy reinforcements [fig. 16].

It was on the 18th [*actually the 17th*] of September, 1864, that Gen. Early marched down to Martinsburg [West Virginia], but finding that Sheridan had gone by another road and was moving on Winchester, retraced his steps by a forced march back to Winchester, arriving there at daylight, just in time to meet Sheridan on the morning of the 20th [*actually the 19th, in the third battle of Winchester, in which Union forces outnumbered the Confederates almost four to one*].[35]

Winchester was a quaint old town of five thousand inhabitants, settled originally mainly by Germans, and was the key to the great Shenandoah Valley. [*Winchester, junction of a number of highways and the*

CHAPTER 6

Fig. 16. "Sheridan's Army in the Shenandoah." From *Harper's Weekly*, 1864, p. 681.

end station of the Winchester and Potomac Railroad, was the northern gateway to the valley.] It was to this point that Gen. Joseph E. Johnston[36] fell back from Harper's Ferry in 1861, three days before the first great battle of Manassas, July 21st, 1861. Gen. Stonewall Jackson was the next Confederate general to occupy Winchester, and here in this famous valley he subsequently made his name famous throughout the world as one of the greatest military leaders of ancient or modern times. It may be truthfully said that Jackson's plans and the execution of them just before the battle of the Wilderness [May 2, 1863] above Richmond will compare favorably with any military achievement ever accomplished by mortal man. With his keen sense of the value of time, he made rapid marches to meet the Federal commands in the Valley whilst they were trying to form a junction to crush him, took them in detail and defeated them all, and then made a forced march for the Wilderness and surprised both the Federal and Confederate armies by opening on McClellan's[37] rear.

Gen. Early met Gen. Sheridan in an old field near Winchester about sunrise [September 19], and for several hours the fight was most stubborn. [*Breckinridge's forces, which, on RGC's witness, still included the Fifty-ninth Tennessee, had been encamped at Stephenson's Depot, an important Confederate supply center on the Potomac and Strasburg branch of the Baltimore and Ohio Railroad, and northeast of Winchester.*[38] *They spent the morning protecting the northern perimeter of the battle area, while Early contended with Sheridan's main force nearer Winchester. Late in the morning Breckinridge encountered Union cavalry under Brigadier General Wesley Merritt near the Opequon Creek and fought off a number of fierce enemy charges. Although there is no official record of mounted troops among the units with Breckinridge in this action, if the Fifty-ninth was there it was now mounted and would have been sent against the enemy cavalry (fig. 17).*] Charges and counter charges were continued up to the afternoon, at which time our artillery had gained a point about where the enemy's artillery had opened in the morning, the killed and wounded then being in our rear. [*On Early's orders, Breckinridge gradually brought his troops in toward Winchester to reinforce those of Major General S. Dodson Ramseur, arriving about 2 P.M. This decision on Early's part may have cost him the day, because the Union successes began at Stephenson's Depot where Merritt joined with other Federal units to form a solid wall that moved ever south to Winchester.*][39] Just at this time Gen. Sheridan succeeded in throwing a heavy force in our rear by a flank movement [*about 3 P.M., under General Crook*], and for a while it was almost impossible to tell from my position which line was Yankees and which was Rebels, so thick was the dust and so great the confusion.[40]

In this battle we were defeated, and Gen. Early fell back up the Valley to Fisher's Hill [*Virginia, after Early decided that Hupp's Hill, north of Strasburg, Virginia, could too easily be flanked. Moreover, breastworks were already in place on the long stretches of Fisher's Hill (fig. 18).*][41] According to the official report, our loss amounted to six thousand men, and the Federals lost five thousand, including many officers of high rank.[42] General Rhodes,[43] one of our ablest division commanders, was killed in this bloody conflict. [*To add to Confederate woes, Breckinridge had been*

CHAPTER 6

Fig. 17. Cavalry action at the Battle of Third Winchester (Currier and Ives, "The Great Victory in the Shenandoah Valley, Va., Sept. 19th 1864"). Courtesy of the Museum of the City of New York, Harry T. Peters Collection.

ordered to another command and had left on the 21st.[44] *Fisher's Hill was highly defensible with sufficient forces, but Early now had fewer than 10,000 effectives, and his line along the extended heights was thin.*[45]] Gen. Sheridan moved upon us on the 2[2]nd of September at Fisher's Hill, evidently with the intention of giving us another blow before we could recover from the defeat at Winchester, and we were again driven back with considerable loss. I was ordered at this point [that is, on the 21st] with a detachment of the brigade to take charge of a picket line nearly a mile in front of our battle lines, and [I] having fought the Yankee pickets all night and all day, Col. Bean, who was in command of the brigade,[46] came out late in the afternoon and promised to relieve me that night. This was welcome news, for I was almost worn out, but such was not to be my good luck. Later on he again visited me and expressed his regret at having to impose so much upon me, but remarked that the enemy would certainly attack us that night or early in the morning, and that he could not supply my place with an officer satisfactory to himself. Early in the morning [September 22] Sheridan

Fig. 18. Fisher's Hill, Virginia. From Johnson and Buel, eds., *Battles and Leaders of the Civil War* 2: 290.

advanced and opened a hot fire upon my lines [on the left]. It was evident they were coming for a general engagement. We were returning the fire as rapidly as possible when one of my men called my attention to the fact that the Confederate pickets on my right had given way and were in full retreat, and the Federal lines were charging parallel with mine. I gave orders to fall back at once in order, and in the retreat we were exposed to a galling fire, losing several men. Among the wounded in this skirmish was my faithful corporal, Croft McCarty,[47] who was carried off soon after the firing began, and I took his gun and pistol and used them to the end of the fight.

Soon after we [*Vaughn's brigade and contingents of Confederate cavalry*][48] fell back into the general battle line on the extreme left, the Yankees began making movements over the hills in heavy columns to charge our position. We repulsed them several times on the left, and notwithstanding our discouraging defeat at Winchester, it began to look as if we would be successful in this battle. Gen. Sheridan, however, got in another one of his flank movements [*using two divisions under General George Crook] by going along the mountain side [Little North Mountain] and striking our left in the rear*—a movement that was not discovered until they were quietly marching up within a few steps behind us.[49] The first I knew of it was when one of my command said "Look here, Captain, behind us!" I ordered my men to turn and fire on the troops coming up in the rear, firing the first shot myself. Casting my eye along the whole line I saw that the Confederate forces were in full retreat, and we then fell back to Harris[on]burg [*Virginia, about fifty miles southwest of Winchester. Only part of Early's forces stopped at Harrisonburg.*[50] *Evidently Vaughn's troops were dismounted in this battle, like those of Brigadier General L. L. Lomax,*[51] *which would explain the episode with the loose horse, described in the following paragraphs. On approaching Harrisonburg, Early's army left the pike, turned eastward, and encamped at the foot of the Blue Ridge Mountains to rest, wait for stragglers, and reorganize.*[52] *One soldier reported that from the camp the Confederates could see the results of the Federal scorched-earth policy:* "the whole valley before our eyes was filled with smoke of burning houses, haystacks, shocks of corn . . . while the crack of carbines brought to our ears the destruction of all farm animals" *(fig. 14)*[53]].

Many horrible and thrilling scenes were witnessed in these trying and perilous times. A full account might be of interest if time and space would allow, but I will only mention a few in this connection as I vividly remember in our hasty retreat from Fisher's Hill. A very excellent young man, Lieut. Davis,[54] had been badly wounded, and his captain and brother were just in front of me, supporting and endeavoring to get him off the field. Young Davis was mortally wounded and was sending his mother his last message. Said he, "Tell my mother that I made a faithful soldier, and died a Christian." Just at this moment a cannon ball struck him in the back, knocking him out of the arms of his kind captain, and he was left a mangled corpse.

At Harris[on]burg [*actually Mount Jackson*][55] that night, worn out and fatigued beyond measure, I got off my horse, and lying on the ground with bridle in hand, was fast asleep in a few moments. Feeling a pressure on me, I woke up to find that Enoch Beeler,[56] one of my company—and, by the way, one of the best soldiers that ever marched to martial music—had lain down by me and placed his head on my body. Said he, "Captain, I feel very badly; I feel that something terrible is going to happen to me." This premonition on his part did not excite my particular interest at the time, and I went back to sleep. Next morning [September 23] we moved up and crossed the [north fork of the Shenandoah] river just as the Federals moved on us and began firing. [*Sheridan followed Early's forces through September 25.*]⁵⁷ We had delivered one round in return when poor Enoch Beeler fell dead, shot in the center of his forehead.

In our retreat from Fisher's Hill, being among the very hindmost men with the infantry, the Federal cavalry passed within a few steps of me and I supposed there was no alternative but to surrender. Just at this moment a Confederate soldier came running by us on horseback, and also leading a horse, when suddenly the horse that was being led took the opposite side of a tree and the young man was of course compelled to let him go. At this juncture the young man with me caught the horse and we both mounted, riding out some three miles through the woods into a little side valley, where we found some artillery officers partaking of a very inviting supper in a farm yard. They had not been in the engagement and appeared to be taking things easy. I left the young man in charge of the horse and went in to ask for something to eat, being almost starved, but was refused; and when I got back to the gate a lieutenant of the artillery company had left the table and was claiming the horse. I said to him that I had been fighting day and night without anything to eat until I was completely worn out, and to walk out was simply out of the question. I also gave him my name and command, saying that I would take care of his horse and deliver it to him after getting out of the way of the enemy. His reply was: "I can't agree to that, Captain; I must have my horse." I said: "Lieutenant, it is rather a desperate case with me; I must ride. Besides, we saved your horse from being captured by the Yankees. I claim to be an honorable man, having told you that I certainly would return you your horse; now I say to you that I can not walk, am broken down, and am sorry to have to take extreme measures, but must say that I will ride this horse out *or die in the attempt!*" He replied, "Well, Captain, if you take that position, the horse will have to go with you." I went out in safety, and returned the horse the next day when I arrived at Staunton [Virginia].

The campaign of the Valley of Virginia was a very fatiguing and trying one, and scarcely a day passed that there was not some fighting. I was in a great many small engagements with the Yankees that it would make it tedious to give an account of. [*Daniel Wesley Long, a private in Clark's Company I, confirms that his outfit fought almost every day, and that "for 3 weeks the horses were not unsaddled except against orders, and we slept in battle line."* He said the men received rations once a day and slept on the ground.][58] Some very sad experiences resulted from these engagements, and sometimes there were others quite amusing. On one occasion [probably July 19, 1864] my regiment was camped in a grove near Darksville [Virginia], between Winchester and Martinsburg. A young lady of that little town, Miss Broughton[59] by name, had invited Capt. John Van Dyke[60] and myself to dine with her. [*It was a common practice for local families to offer meals to the troops and to invite officers to their tables.*][61] We had just finished dinner and returned to the parlor when another young lady, living across the street, and whose acquaintance we had formed, came to the window and cried out: "The Yankees are charging into town!" We had heard the musketry and had supposed it was the usual picket firing, which was a daily occurrence and in which we often engaged, ourselves, so thought little of it; but when the young lady spoke, we both sprang to our feet and hurried to reach our commands. Our army had moved off up the valley and left our regiment unsupported—a movement of which we had not been informed—and the Yankees, having observed it, charged on us, expecting to capture the regiment. We had but fairly reached the command, then in line, when the Federals charged furiously upon us, and the gallant little captain, John Van Dyke, fell mortally wounded into the hands of one of my men, Samuel Hickle.[62] The boys put him into an ambulance, which carried him up the valley, until the ambulance was overtaken by the enemy and his remains fell into their hands. He was carried back to Darksville that evening and was buried in that town by the same two young ladies referred to on the foregoing page. Thus ended the life of a modest, refined and gallant young gentleman, whom I greatly esteemed. Capt. Van Dyke was a son of Judge Van Dyke, at present a citizen of Rome [Georgia], and he was a brother of Robert Van Dyke, Mrs. George Battey and Mrs. Hugh Inman.[63]

About two weeks after this engagement our brigade was in line across some old fields in the Valley of Virginia, awaiting the approach of the enemy as they were slowly coming in sight; and after remaining in line several hours, Mr. Dick Van Dyke,[64] a brother of the young man who was killed, and myself went to a house near by to get something to eat; and upon our return the Yankees charged on us. In the engagement Major Van Dyke was slightly wounded in the knee—and he laughingly asked me as we went off the field together, "Do you suppose I can get a furlough on this wound?" He was carried back to Lynchburg and there died from the effects of that shot.

These two brothers were fine types of young manhood, handsome, brave and gallant, and they were admired by all the command. I have often thought of the coincidence of having dined for the last time with these two noble brothers and close friends of mine, under the circumstances which I have related.

At another time [probably July 25, 1864][65] the regiment was quartered in the streets of Martinsburg [fig. 19], waiting to ascertain the strength of the enemy beyond the time [*i.e., waiting longer than expected*], when the Federal cavalry made a furious charge on our rear, which threw our regiment into a panic for a moment, and they started to get out by every avenue in any direction. A number of us began crying: "Stop and fight!" when every man turned and a hand-to-hand conflict in the streets ensued. Quite a number were shot, but the Yankee cavalry were completely routed and went out of town in great confusion.[66] The saddest thing in connection with this incident was the killing of a lady and little child.

Martinsburg was a strong Union town and its populace very bitter against the South.

CHAPTER 6

Fig. 19. Confederate Troops at Martinsburg, Virginia. From *Harper's Weekly*, 1864, p. 781.

A few days after this incident I was ordered with my company to relieve Gen. Terry,[67] who was in command of the old Stonewall Brigade, in charge of Martinsburg, about nine miles from the Potomac River [and about sixty miles] above Washington. This old brigade at that time numbered but a few more men than I had in my company. Gen. Terry said to me as I relieved him: "Captain, you will find these people insolent and ready to practice any kind of deception upon you. One of their favorite schemes will be to send your men on Confederate families here to hunt Yankee horses and other property, which they allege belong to Federal officers." Sure enough, on the second day after my arrival, some of my men came in and reported Yankee horses in a stable across the creek, where there was a fine residence. I told them to ascertain who lived there, and they came back and reported that the man's name was Charles J. Faulkner, (a distinguished Virginia rebel). I then instructed the men to pay no attention to reports of that kind from the citizens of that town.

My headquarters were in an old store house on Main Street, and while [I was] sitting out on the pavement, perhaps reading the papers, the young ladies taking their evening walk, frequently made it a point to pass by and say unpleasant things, such as, "Our folks will soon be back and drive these rebels out, and we can have a nice time with our boys, eating ice cream," etc.

After leaving Martinsburg and returning to Winchester, I was ordered to return to Martinsburg and ascertain the strength, movement and position of the enemy. Finding a Federal company stationed in the town, I charged them along the streets, driving them out, and accomplished my purpose without any casualties. [*Martinsburg, on the Valley Pike between Winchester and Hagerstown, Maryland, changed hands frequently.*]

One of the most pleasant experiences I had in this campaign was at Hagerstown, Maryland. My regiment was the advance guard of the army in our invasion of Maryland, and we halted in the outskirts of the city to await further orders [July 30, 1864; fig. 20].[68] Wishing to see what kind of a place it was, I walked along the street making observations, when I met quite a company of young ladies going out, as I supposed, to see how the Rebels looked. I got off the pavement and gave the way when one of the party, who proved to be a Miss Schley,[69] stopped me and asked quite a number of questions while the others looked on. Finally she asked me if I had been to dinner, to which I replied in the negative. She then invited me to accompany them home and take dinner with them. The family I found to be a very charming people. Colonel Schley, a very distinguished lawyer, and his most excellent lady were very hospitable, and their two attractive daughters greatly increased the pleasure of my visit. Mrs. Schley gave me a seat at the table between her two daughters, and a jolly meal we made of it. After dinner Judge Hunter, a brother of Senator Hunter,[70] of Virginia, came in with some company and introduced me to friends. It was almost an ovation. Hagerstown, unlike Martinsburg, was a rebel town. I was introduced to Mr. Hager,[71] a very elegant old gentleman, who entertained me royally, frankly told me that he was a Union man, but he was not blind to the fact that other gentlemen had as much right to their opinion as he on the principle involved

Fig. 20. "Confederate Troops at Hagerstown, Maryland," from a sketch by Theodore R. Davis. From *Harper's Weekly*, 1862, p. 621.

in the war. It always gave him pleasure to meet a gentleman of the other side and frankly interchange views. We had quite an interview, during which he set out his fine wine and cigars, which seemed to be a feature in every house I visited; and when I rose to take leave of him he handed me quite a large package of ground coffee to take with me. [*Coffee was often enjoyed by Federals, but it was a rare treat for a Confederate.*][72] A part of this coffee was in my saddle wallet when I finally surrendered at Morristown. Gen. Early had some prisoners sometime afterwards, which he held as hostages for citizens of Virginia who had been carried out by Gen. Hunter, among whom was Mr. Hager. A gentleman who witnessed the conversation between Mr. Hager and myself came up and appealed to me to make an effort to get Mr. Hager released; and I had started to overtake the command to do what I could for him, when I met the old gentleman on his return, having been released by Gen. Early.

That night we camped between Hagerstown and the Potomac River. Lieut. James King,[73] of Knoxville, who had enjoyed the same kind of hospitality in Hagerstown that I did, at another house, proposed that we get permission to return to Hagerstown and ascertain what the Federals were doing. In reality we cared nothing about the Federals—just so they kept out of our way. Having put out videttes to avoid surprise, we went next morning and found the Yankee picket forces formed across the street at the court house. I told King to charge with his men up through town along the street to the left, and I would charge by the main street. We made a vigorous charge and they opened fire on us, but fled on the first round. We drove them some distance beyond the city, capturing some of their baggage and hats and other plunder, and put out pickets to guard the road; and the Lieutenant and I returned to take breakfast with our respective friends.

It was about sunrise when we made the charge. When I got back to Colonel Schley's the young ladies had not finished dressing. They soon came down, however, and as they entered the parlor the eldest remarked: "I told sister that it was you, when I heard the guns firing." They were certainly charming young ladies. The eldest was a cripple, and used crutches; she is now an old maid, and the organist of the Presbyterian church at Hagerstown. The other sister married soon after the war, and died several years after marriage. These are pleasant memories, and I have continued to exchange messages with this interesting family ever since the war.

It is surprising what a bold charge will accomplish sometimes. I have seen small detachments of Rebels make a charge on five times their number of Yankees and route them; and have seen the Yankees do the same thing, charging Rebels. On one occasion when I was occupying a picket post on a high point in a little valley running parallel with the Valley of Virginia, my brigade commander [Vaughn] ordered me in, as it was understood that the army was going to move down the valley to meet the enemy. When I reached headquarters, however, plans had been changed, and I was ordered to resume my position in the little valley. I suggested that it might be troublesome, as the Yankees were in sight when I left it. But the General gave me no reinforcements, and upon my return I found the post occupied by more than double my strength. As soon as I ascertained that the enemy were in possession of my position, I ordered my men to tear down the fence, saying that we would charge them through the field, which was covered with weeds higher than a person's head, and owing to a rise in the ground within a few rods of the picket forces, it was impossible for them to observe our numbers. I instructed the men to yell louder and longer than they ever did before, as we wanted to whip that crowd before we exposed our numbers. Such awful yelling I have never since heard by so small a detachment. When we reached the top of the hill the Federals were going pell mell down the other side, panic stricken, about one hundred of them; and after they got out of sight they were so badly frightened that they got down and built fences across the road.

I might give accounts of a great many engagements in Virginia, in which my friend, Capt. John Van Dyke, came to my assistance. Always reliable, he never flickered. Another little Confederate captain I may mention here who had often been with me when we were pressed, was Captain Ed Gammon, a brother of the Gammons of this city [Rome, Georgia] and son of the venerable Wm. E. Gammon. Ed was handsome and brave, and as gallant a boy as ever went into a charge. [*In a history of Vaughn's brigade, Captain Ed Gammon is called "one of the most gallant officers of the army."*][74]

After resting up a week or so [*after the Fisher's Hill retreat*], our brigade was ordered back to East Tennessee in October [the 12th or 13th], 1864.[75]

Chapter 7

My company was well acquainted with the route[s] and passways through the mountains and valleys of Tennessee. I was kept much of the time in front of our lines, and sometimes went around the Federal position to ascertain their strength in infantry, cavalry and artillery. In performance of these duties I often came in contact with Federal outposts, composed of East Tennessee Unionists. They were very bitter against me, and threatened dire vengeance in case they captured me. Many of my friends, most of them ladies, sent me word to be sure and not be taken prisoner; that the East Tennesseeans [sic] were going to kill me if I ever fell into their hands.

It was a short time after I returned to East Tennessee from the Valley of Virginia before Gen. Gillam[1] moved up from Knoxville and attacked our brigade at Morristown [October 28, 1864].[2] Gen. Vaughn, then in command of our brigade, stopped at Bull's Gap, the strongest position in that vicinity; but for some reason, which I could never understand, moved on [13 miles southwest] to Morristown to meet Gillam in a broad open field, where they had unlimited space for flank movement with superior numbers. [*The Confederate line was drawn up in two groups across a field to the east and the west of Morristown.*][3] Gen. Vaughn was a brave man, although deficient in military judgement and skill. There were many privates in that brigade that would have made a more successful fight than he did. [*Here RGC reflects a current opinion in the command, but Vaughn would soon do very well, and indeed, routed Gillem at Morristown on November 14.]*[4]

Occupying a high point on our left, from which I could observe the movements of the entire line, I could see that Gen. Gillam was making a fierce charge on our right wing, and to break the force of this charge I appealed to Col. Carter[5] to order a charge on their right, which he did. We drove them back to some extent, but in doing so I noticed that our whole force on the right were in full retreat and passing out of the field. I made an unsuccessful attempt to save our artillery, but as the enemy was too close upon us, that was impossible. Besides, I discovered that the enemy had gotten in our rear, and immediately put my horse out at full speed to pass them. I would have gone through all right but for the unfortunate circumstance of my horse striking a stump and falling to the ground with my foot under him. I came up with him, however, as he rose, but minus saddle, hat and baggage. [*The Confederate defeat at Morristown was reported with delight by Knoxville's Unionist editor, William G. Brownlow (fig. 3).*][6]

I succeeded in getting into a skirt of woods close by, but by this time the Yankees were on all sides, and I was completely surrounded. A young man in front of me shot Lieut. Bell[7] in the side just as he ran his horse in between us. The young man made his escape, and I was made a prisoner. Bell thought it was I who shot him, and was making at me with uplifted sword, when Colonel Jo Parsons[8] galloped up and stopped him, saying, "You might be a prisoner yourself some day!" I recognized Parsons promptly, and in this supreme moment of my peril decided to make the best use of him possible. Colonel Parsons had been a candidate for Congress in the Knoxville district before the war. My brother [?John], who at that time was often taken for me, was one of his strongest supporters, travelling with him in his campaign and making speeches for him on many occasions, but Parsons was defeated by a small majority by Colonel Sneed,[9] whom I supported. Turning to Colonel Parsons I said, "I believe I have had the honor of meeting Colonel Parsons." "Yes," said he, "but I do not remember you." I said, "Clark is my name; I once had the pleasure of supporting you for Congress, as you may remember." Parsons replied that he remembered me and was very glad to meet me again, but sorry that it was under such circumstances. My scheme worked well. Colonel Parsons ordered one of his men to saddle a horse and bring [it] to me, and calling a lieutenant, told him to accompany me to Morristown and allow me to provide myself with such articles as I needed, hat, etc., and get my dinner among friends. He also told the lieutenant that I was a gentleman and a friend of his. These instructions to the men who had me in charge proved invaluable. I could hear some of the East Tennessee men cursing me, and expressing the wish that they could get a shot at me, but the officer in charge rebuked them, and I arrived in Knoxville the next day in company with about one hundred and sixty other prisoners.[10]

On the evening of the fight we were marched to Mossy Creek [now Jefferson City, Tennessee] to remain for the night, Lieut. Nelson,[11] in charge, still guarding me. He granted me the privilege of going into the house of one of my friends, and it was here that I met some of the young ladies who had sent me the message "never to be captured." They were daughters of Doctor Rhoten,[12] strong Rebels, and very attractive. They seemed to be greatly distressed, and cried bitterly.

One rather singular fact in connection with my war experience was that I went into camp after first making up a company at Morristown; and after fighting in the different departments of the Southern Confederacy, from the Potomac to the Mississippi, I was captured at that same Morristown.

Thus ended my career as a soldier *in the field*.

This same Lieut. Nelson was a prisoner in my charge very early in the contest, and his father was my attorney at the close of the war, when they were prosecuting me for treason.

Chapter 8

It is said: "The unexpected always happens." Little did I expect to be a prisoner in the hands of those East Tennessee Federals; but it was a sad reality—and here begins by far the worst part of my war experience.

I thought the Vicksburg campaign about as trying in all its details as any experience short of being mortally wounded could be, [and] when I was in line of battle at Virginia, fighting day in and day out, many times with nothing to eat for days, until I could scarcely put one foot before the other, my comrades falling all round me before the deadly fire of the enemy. I thought no experience could be worse than that, short of death; but those days were a paradise compared to the ordeal through which I was destined to pass in the Knoxville prison. The Federals have claimed credit for kind treatment to prisoners during the war between the States, but I know both through experience and observation, that this claim is based on fiction. Prison life under any circumstances is hard, but when persecutions are added to the ordinary trials to which a prisoner of war is subjected, it is simply horrible. We have heard much of Andersonville [Georgia] Prison, and doubtless the privations and sufferings of prisoners at that place were very great; but great as they were, they have been much exaggerated when we take into consideration that the Confederate authorities, being hard pressed to supply our men, offered to exchange the prisoners at Andersonville, and failing in that, offered to parole them and let them go home if the Federal authorities would furnish them with transportation, and the further fact that the Confederate authorities made every proposition possible, to get them to take the prisoners off our hands. But regardless of the sufferings and privations of their men, they persistently allowed them to remain at Andersonville, with no other purpose than to continue that large body of Yankee soldiers on our hands in order to help deplete our almost exhausted supplies of provisions. In view of these facts we are led to ask the question: "Which side was responsible for the suffering of the prisoners at Andersonville?" Perhaps fifty or [one] hundred years from now, not less, impartial history will give the unvarnished truth on these matters, and let the blame fall where it belongs.[1]

I was a prisoner in the hands of my own East Tennessee people, largely controlled by civic and military leaders, who were bitter and vindictive beyond measure. In fact, the bitter feelings between the East Tennesseeans—who were about equally divided between the north and the south—was more intense than it was between any other sections or commands. On the first morning after we arrived in Knoxville [October 30, 1864] the prisoners were called out, and all who had no charges preferred against them were sent to northern prisons, while the rest of us were kept in the Knoxville jail [*used for Confederate military prisoners and Union criminals*[2]] [fig. 4]. Upon [my] entering the jail the prison sergeant turned and ordered me to follow him up stairs, where he unlocked a small iron cage and ordered me to step inside [fig. 5].[3] To this place the Federal officers and citizens as well would come and glare at me through the iron bars, as though I were a monster. I wrote to Gen. Carter,[4] then in command of the Federal forces at Knoxville, to be informed as to the cause of my being detained and subjected to extraordinary treatment. He replied that I was charged with murder, and would be tried on that charge as soon as a military commission could be organized.

The next morning Brownlow's *Knoxville Whig and Rebel Ventilator* came out with a column devoted to my case, in which he charged

CHAPTER 8

that I had caused Major Gray to be shot after he had surrendered, and urged that I be taken out and shot by a mob.

[*Brownlow's article reads as follows:*

Captain Reuben Clark

This man used to be a clerk in the store of Cowan & Dickinson where he was better educated than to play the bushwacker in the rebel service. He is the young man who stripped Capt. Gray, formerly of the First Tennessee Cavalry [USA], chained him to a tree and riddled his body with bullets. This was done a few miles west of Rogersville [Tennessee], and can be proven upon Clark. The cold-blooded assassin was captured last Friday by Gen. Gillem's command and is now in one of the iron cages in this city.

Such a man ought never to be exchanged as a prisoner of war or sent North to a military prison. Our authorities owe it to the memory of the gallant Capt. Gray, they owe it to the First Tennessee Cavalry [USA], and to the cause of humanity, as well as the Confederate cause, to try this man by court martial and execute him on the spot where he murdered Gray.][5]

A few days after I was put into the cage, some one handed me some Cincinnati and New York papers, in which my capture was announced, and also saying that I would probably be executed for killing a Federal officer.[6] I also received a Richmond paper, which made mention of my capture and the charges preferred against me, the article stating that if extreme measures were resorted to in my case, Gen. Breckenridge would retaliate by subjecting a Federal officer of my rank to the same treatment. [*The* Richmond Enquirer, *the principal Confederate newspaper, for November 15, 1864, p. 3, had the following:*

Capt. Reuben Clark, who was captured by the enemy at Morristown, has been sentenced to be executed in twenty days by the authorities at Knoxville. It is pretended that Capt. Clark is implicated in the killing of a Union man by the name of Gray, from Grainger county, but which charge we understand to be wholly false. Should they carry out this order, no doubt the strictest retaliation will be resorted to by the Confederate authorities.

A deed so foul and barbarous should not be submitted to for a single moment without the full power of the government being invoked to retaliate. The lex talionis is a desperate remedy, but must be resorted to in cases like the present.][7]

I then wrote to Gen. Carter, calling his attention to these articles and asking an early investigation, as there were persons then within the Federal lines of responsibility who were with me at that time and who knew the charges to be false. To this appeal I received no reply, but was kept in prison eight months and then turned over to the civil authorities to be tried for treason against the government of the United States. I never was called before a court martial.

While in this prison I was served with a warrant confiscating all my property, and in my helpless situation, made a mistake that cost me all that I possessed. [*It is possible that this too was at Brownlow's instigation. In 1863 he was appointed U.S. Treasury agent for East Tennessee, a post which he used regularly to punish Rebels, or even suspected Rebels, by confiscating their property. Because until May 1864 there was no civil court at Knoxville, nothing could be done to curb Brownlow's excesses.*][8] I wrote a note to George Mayo, who had been my partner in business, informing him of the fact and requesting him to protect himself on financial matters. We owned some tobacco jointly, which was stored in Lynchburg, and on this account Mayo brought suit against me for twenty five thousand dollars, obtained judgement and defeated the confiscation of my property by the Government—just the course I desired him to give the matter. But in the meantime Mayo became badly involved by reason of a dangerous mistake in his own business affairs, and before I could have my property conveyed back to myself, which was part of my plans, his creditors captured my property and I was left without any recourse. [*RGC's business partnership with George*

Mayo seems also to have involved real estate. Part of the property lost through Mayo's error was two lots of land that RGC and Mayo had bought from William A. and H. L. Spencer in December 1862, and which were later seized by confiscation. Legal proceedings began in District Court on January 4, 1865, when the case was continued. On January 10, 1866, Clark was permitted to file a plea of pardon, which was finally heard on June 22, 1866. The court found that the Confiscation Law had not gone into effect until after the conveyance of the properties to Clark and Mayo. Thus, Mayo could now legally reconvey to RGC the latter's half of the ownership. Taxes and court costs, the latter in the then substantial amount of $245, were levied from Clark and Mayo at a hearing on May 31, 1867, and a lien was retained on the property until the taxes were paid.][9]

Thus, from owning a nice estate, I was made practically penniless by Mayo's blunder, who was acting in perfect good faith to protect me whilst I had no opportunity to look after my own interest. If I had allowed the authorities to confiscate my property without protesting, and had paid no attention to the court proceedings, I would have sustained no loss, as the court proceedings were altogether illegal and were subsequently made void by the Supreme court. This seemed very hard luck to me, for I was utterly helpless.

The winter was distressingly severe, the prison poorly supplied with fuel; there were no shutters in the windows, and it was about as cold inside as out. I found it necessary to exert myself in various ways to keep from freezing. One way was to hold my boot straps and jump up and down in the cage. I had a piece of meat issued to me daily that would not grease the water in which it was boiled, and a little hard tack. [*By contrast, during the time that Clark's nemesis "Parson" Brownlow spent in the Knoxville jail, he "was allowed the privilege of having my meals sent from home three times each day."*][10]

General Breckenridge had sent down a flag of truce, demanding to know what my treatment was, and informed Gen. Carter that he would subject a Federal officer of my rank to the same treatment I received.[11] Gen. Morgan subsequently did the same thing,[12] and to both Gen. Carter replied, in order to save his own men, that I should be treated as other prisoners of war. I wrote to the general commanding, asking him to allow my friends to furnish me with something to eat.[13] This was peremptorily denied, the adjutant-general replying that the last information he had from Andersonville prison was that the men were then getting a pint of meal for two days rations, with no salt to put in it. I wrote again to Gen. Carter, asking nothing for myself but calling his attention to the fact that the Confederate prisoners were being carried out daily in pine boxes, who were dying from cold and starvation, including in my appeal the name of an old man, (Perry),[14] an uncle of Gen. Carter himself, who was suffering greatly in an iron cage near the one in which I was confined. The Confederates were huddled on the floor in the open jail building, without blankets and very thinly clad, and without fire, when the winter was intensely cold. The only response to my appeal to Gen. Carter was some allusion to Andersonville and a bottle of whiskey sent old man Perry.[15]

In this extremity I tried to cultivate the sergeants and some other Federals that came into the prison, thinking that it might be possible to excite their sympathy to the extent of obtaining through them a little something to eat that would be nourishing; but all my politeness and humiliation went for nothing. They were a set of flints, blinded by the prejudiced influences around them, and I could no more impress them than I could a stone. In fact, the whole Brownlow gang were for persecuting me, and there was no alternative but to submit. They would not even allow my friends to see me, much less to furnish me with food or clothing. I wrote to a number of friends for different articles, such as an overcoat, blankets, etc., but received no response. After my release I learned that but few of the notes were delivered, and that the articles which were sent to the provost marshall's offices for me were returned to the senders, with the remark by the marshall that "Capt. Clark was a very bad man, and could not have them." Among the articles sent to the marshall's office was an overcoat by Mr. D[ickinson], in whose employ I had been.

The marshall [*probably Ed Trigg*] was a little "swell German Major" and "petty tyrant," who lodged in Knoxville when hostilities ceased, and is still residing there.

The outlaws of the Federal army were kept in the same prison with the Confederate prisoners, and the filth and vermin, to say nothing of the other horrors of the place, were perfectly awful;[16] indeed, it is useless to undertake to give in detail an account of the persecutions inflicted upon Confederate soldiers and sympathizers in Knoxville and vicinity. Brownlow had command of the mob, and men were shot down like dogs.

I will give one instance to illustrate. There was an old gentleman, whose name I can not remember—having lost my notes, in consequence of which I have been unable to give dates and details throughout this sketch as I desired to do—this old gentleman came into the prison and on the first day sought me to say that the Federal authorities were threatening vengeance against me. This, of course, was no news to me, but as he seemed to be a clever, inoffensive old man, I was glad to talk with him. For this he was arrested for treason, and upon a brief investigation Judge Trigg[17] released him on bond. Brownlow came out in his paper next morning, denouncing the court for having released the prisoner on bond, with the advice that as the court would not do him justice, it remained for the Union soldiers who had been driven from their homes to see that he got justice; that he and all other amnestied scoundrels like him should die—should die quietly, but die surely![18] The next heard of this old gentleman, he was found dead, with nine musket ball holes in his body—the result, doubtless, of Mr. Brownlow's advice.

To say that all Union people sympathized with this mob spirit would do great injustice, for there were many leading citizens who deplored the cruelties perpetrated upon Confederates, and did much for their protection. This class of citizens had the manliness to live above prejudice and passion, and received back to their homes and firesides the friends of former days who differed with them on this question. In other words, they unhesitatingly resumed friendly relations with the men who had gone into the southern army, while the majority seemed to be with the mob.

Brownlow was a candidate for governor, and in his speeches told the Union soldiers of East Tennessee that the Rebels who had driven out the loyal citizens, as he alleged, should be killed, and if the Union soldiers were convicted of murder for killing the Rebels that he, as governor, would meet them at the door of the penitentiary and turn them loose. This was about the close of the war, and upon such utterances he was overwhelmingly elected [1865] to the gubernatorial chair.

One style of amusement indulged in by the Union people was to horsewhip Rebels who had returned to their homes unarmed and helpless. These lawless acts of oppression drove many of the best citizens out of the country, and today East Tennessee Confederates are scattered over every state in the Union.[19] One of the bitterest men in Knoxville was the Hon. Horace Maynard,[20] a Massachusetts Yankee, who came to Knoxville and taught school, then became a lawyer, and for many years represented the Knoxville district in Congress, and was afterwards minister to Turkey under Gen. Grant. My father had always given him a loyal support, and I myself travelled with him in his canvasses for Congress, and worked for him as true as I ever did for any one in my life; but this counted for nothing, and he declined to speak to me after the war. Nothing seemed to be so much to his liking as to abuse and oppress his former friends who differed with him on the issue of secession. He was a cold blooded Yankee, full of vengeance, and shut into his own narrow self with his bitterness and prejudices. On one occasion when the Federal court was in session, Maynard, who was always in some broil with the bar of East Tennessee, made a speech in which he denounced Rebels generally, and insisted that it should be made a rule of the court that no attorney should be allowed to practice who could not take the "iron clad oath"; in other words, who had not remained loyal to the government of the United States during the war. Hon. Thomas A. R. Nelson,[21] a very able man and also a very strong Union man, but without Maynard's bitterness, and one who loved justice, got up to reply to Maynard's speech, and the fire in his eye indicated clearly to those who knew him what was coming. He spoke five hours, but I will only give a few sentences by which the rest of his speech may be judged. Turning to the court, he said: "I thank my God that I was reared in these hills, that I imbibed the pure atmosphere of these mountains, and have the manhood of my own convictions. These gentlemen, with whom I have long been associated, are my brothers; they are honorable men, and our differences have been honest differences." Then turning to Maynard, who had taken his seat, said, with his finger pointing near his face, "Sir, whenever I become so low, so despicable, so sunk beneath the brute creation, as to come back from the bleak and barren hills of Massachusetts, among a people who had taken me from poverty and destitution, supported and encouraged me, trusted and elevated me to place and power, when I come back to that people in the gaudy robes of victory and undertake to elbow myself into their practice by the subterfuge of abominable test-oaths, may God Almighty cause my perjured tongue to cleave to the roof of my filthy mouth, and may I be buried in the grave of infamy so deep that Gabriel's trumpet can never reach my polluted ear!" This is a fair sample of his five hour speech on the Hon. Horace Maynard. [*This long, colorful quotation suggests that either RGC heard Nelson's speech or had access to a transcript of it.*]

Before dismissing the distinguished gentleman to whom these two pages are dedicated, it may be proper to say that just before the war Mr. Maynard, then a member of Congress, was in correspondence with my friend, P. M. McClung,[22] of Knoxville. Mr. McClung was a very enthusiastic Whig and a strong Rebel, believing, as he did, that Tennessee was going to vote for the ordinance of secession and that our people were all going that way. He doubtless impressed Maynard with that belief, and Maynard, taking it for granted that McClung was right, in order to be on the strong side made a violent speech in Congress against the north, in which he told them they could never conquer the south.[23] In other words, his speech sounded like a southern "Fire-eater." As it turned out, Tennessee went by an overwhelming majority at the first election against secession, and many of Maynard's friends remonstrated with him on his Washington speech. To make amends honorably, or, to put it plainly, to get back on the right side, Maynard then made the most foolish, as well as the most heartless speech ever uttered by a southern man. Said he: "Rather than see this Union disrupted, I would see my wife dishonored before my eyes, and my children torn limb from limb to pieces!!"[24] Mr. Nelson doubtless had this in mind when he thanked his God that he had the manhood of his own convictions.

Among the first citizens of Knoxville who aided the Union side, it is gratifying to be able to say that there were many who opposed the proscriptive policy of such men as Brownlow and Maynard. These gentlemen, among whom it gives me pleasure to mention Judge Trigg, Col. Baxter, Mr. Dickinson, Mr. Cowan, Col. John Williams, Gen. Kyle[25] and others, did a great deal to ameliorate the hardships of the Confederate prisoners, and without their influence that section would have been but little less than a human slaughter pen.

Under pressure of exposure, cold and hunger, I had to succumb to sickness. Dr. Leonard [fig. 21],[26] of the Federal command, was called to see me and visited me several times, when one of my fellow prisoners said to him, "Doctor, Captain Clark ought to be carried to the hospital; if kept here, he is going to die." The doctor made some evasive answer. Almost too weak to talk, I said, "Doctor, I suppose the reason you do not admit me to the hospital is because charges have been preferred against me." His reply was, "Yes, Captain, that it is."

Replying I said to him that I was aware of the charges of Brownlow, and that they were false; though I could not expect him to act upon my statement, yet as an act of simple justice to a helpless, sick prisoner, I would ask him to go to Gen. Carter and say to him that I was fully posted [*probably through the prison grapevine*] as to the correspondence between himself and

CHAPTER 8

Fig. 21. Dr. Charles Leonard, Tenth Michigan Cavalry, USA. Photograph courtesy of the U.S. Army Michigan Cavalry 10th Regiment, Bentley Historical Library, Univ. of Michigan, Ann Arbor.

the Confederate authorities respecting my case; that if he imagined he was deceiving me, or any one else, he was making a grave mistake; that I had already fully informed Gen. Breckenridge of his duplicity, and that he would doubtless hear again from that gentleman at an early date. It took me a long time to express these matters, as I was almost too weak to talk. The Doctor paid very close attention, however, and seemed greatly interested. When I finished he quietly went out without saying anything in reply. In a short time he was back with a detail of men and a stretcher to carry me to the hospital [January 14, 1865],[27] going along himself to superintend my moving. He had me well covered up, and I could hear the ladies along the way, notably at Dr. Park's [*Tennessee School for the Deaf, converted into a hospital*],[28] saying, "I wonder if that is poor Captain Clark?"

Dr. Leonard became very much interested in my behalf, and gave me every possible attention, especially during the first two weeks, when my life seemed to be hanging in the balance. My illness came from a complication of ailments, and even after I was able to sit up, erysipelas[29] broke out all over my face and head and was so severe that my hair had to be shaved off; and with the most diligent and careful attention the doctor could give me, my friends were very apprehensive that my illness would prove fatal. My eyes swollen until closed, and my head shaved— I presented a frightful appearance. I will not undertake here to describe my sufferings from that sickness—they were simply indescribable. The Yankee doctor was a very hard swearer, and when he would come in and discover that the malady had broken over the limit of his application, and seemed to defy his diligent doctoring, he would swear like a sailor. He finally brought me up, however, and I was fully restored to my former health.

In the meantime more flags of truce had been sent down, based on a communication that I had sent to Gen. Breckenridge sewed up in a Confederate's coat collar, who was carried out of prison to be exchanged. [*This refers probably to the letter seen in late January 1865 by Robert Ould, Confederate exchange agent, as noted in the Introduction.*] About this time a very handsome little sergeant, (a courier at Gen. Carter's headquarters), turned to one of my fellow prisoners and said: "I have heard a great deal of Captain Clark, and want to see him; the Confederate generals are making a big fuss about him." [*RGC's cagemate, Captain John*] Reynolds brought him to me and introduced him. He had a fine, handsome face, and after quite a conversation, went out, having impressed me very pleasantly. [*As noted in the Introduction, Reynolds was allowed daily periods outside the cage.*]

This gentlemanly little Yankee sergeant became a warm friend, and rendered me special service in various ways. He was the medium through whom my beautiful and charming little friend, Miss Mary Alexander,[30] and I conducted a secret correspondence about my case, which finally resulted in her employment of Hon. Thomas A. R.

Nelson, Judge John Baxter and Col. John Netherland to defend me.[31] My little Yankee friend kept faith with us to the last, and became a great favorite with all Confederates who found him out. He and my good doctor were the only Federal officers from whom I ever received any consideration or kindness during my eight months confinement, and it was truly refreshing to meet them.

Dr. Leonard became a warm friend and was very companionable, spending much time playing whist with me in the hospital, and sometimes remaining through the night, having provided me with a commodious bed. My friends were permitted to see me and furnish me with eatables, cigars, etc., etc. Many of the very nicest people in the city often called to see me, and furnished me with more nice delicacies than I could dispose of. The Doctor naturally noticed what class of people were calling and sending supplies, and upon one occasion sent his sergeant to the hospital after me, requesting that I come out of prison and dine with him. It was on that occasion that he cursed out Brownlow and all his sort, remarking that he, (the Doctor), knew the difference between a gentleman and a blackguard, regardless of which side he was on. He even went so far as to say that if I would be very careful to avoid getting him into trouble, I might disguise myself and visit at night the young ladies who had been calling at the hospital to see me. But upon reflection we both decided that this would be unwise, both from his standpoint and mine; for if discovered, it might give us trouble.

At bed time that night I left him in his comfortable quarters, after partaking of his good dinner, returning unattended to the hospital; and whilst I might have easily made my escape by abusing his confidence, the adherents of Brownlow were saying to my friends that I would most surely be executed.

After recovering my health I enjoyed to the fullest extent, under Dr. Leonard's liberal treatment, the visits of kind friends and the superabundance of good things with which they supplied me. So delightful was it, compared with my jail experience that I would then have considered it no hardship, with such pleasant surroundings, to have remained there forever. Among the many kind friends who helped to relieve my hardships of prison life, I would mention the name of Mrs. Isabella French,[32] a widow, who was indeed a mother to me. She was a charming woman, greatly beloved by all who knew her, and was always doing good. She had applied to headquarters to be permitted to furnish me with meals before I was removed to the hospital, and was refused. But after my removal, she was successful in her application to Doctor Leonard, and upon her first visit to the hospital she seemed as glad to see me as if I had been her own son. She furnished me with food regularly for six or eight weeks, and was distressed beyond measure when they took me back to jail. As she afterwards told me, she thought then they were going to execute me. Kind, gentle and refined, she was almost idolized by the young people who visited her hospitable home.

Doubtless you may wish to know who Mrs. French was. Her maiden name was Miss White, daughter of Hugh Lawson White, a distinguished senator from Tennessee with Clay, Webster and Calhoun, and was defeated for president of the United States in 1836 by Gen. [Andrew] Jackson.[33] Georgia, among others, voted for White. At the approach of the next presidential election the Whigs, under the leadership of Gen. Harrison,[34] nominated Judge White, but by this time his health had failed and he could not accept the nomination.

After my final release from prison, finding that Mrs. French had lost about all except her home, I stepped into the store of a friend who kept a wholesale grocery establishment and requested him to send a dray [cart] load of supplies, including a barrel of sugar, a sack of coffee and such other articles as she was likely to need, to Mrs. French, and under no circumstances to let her know who sent them. I was only too glad to do this out of my meagre supply of greenback. I was sometimes amused at her efforts to find out who had sent the supplies, and it was about two years before she succeeded. Mrs. French is dead now—God bless her memory! She was a lovely woman.

On one occasion the field officer of the day came into the hospital to escort me to the gate to meet three of the handsomest young ladies in Tennessee, Misses Ella Cocke, Mary and Fannie Alexander—the latter, sisters of Maj. Charles Alexander, previously referred to.[35] The officer was evidently struck with the beauty of the young ladies and remained for quite a while, during which time he made several ineffectual attempts to engage them in conversation. Finally he submitted the proposition to Miss Mary Alexander, that would it not be better for me to give up the Confederate cause, which was then hopeless, take the oath of allegiance and save my property [*as large numbers of Confederates did when prisoners of war*]. I can never forget the expression of her beautiful dark eyes as she turned them upon him and said: "Do you suppose, sir, that a southern gentleman would stigmatize his name by deserting his country's cause?"[36] The effect was overwhelming; the Yankee bowed himself out and was gone.

Chapter 9

I was sitting in the hospital one beautiful morning, thinking, as all my friends did, that the worst of my prison experience was over, that my persecutors had relaxed somewhat in their bitterness toward me, and that I would probably be released without being carried back to jail. In this I was sadly mistaken, however, as it was on that morning that Doctor Leonard came and said to me, "Captain Clark, I have a painful duty to perform this morning," at the same time handing me a paper that read: "Doctor Leonard: You will return Captain R. G. Clark to prison immediately under a strong guard." I signified my readiness to go, and was placed between two rows of soldiers and marched back to jail [*but not to the iron cage, for later he mentions walking to his bunk*]. This was a surprise to my friends as well as myself, as we did not understand what it meant. I could see my prison friends in groups, discussing the matter quietly among themselves.

Next morning Brownlow announced in his paper that a Federal recruiting officer, who was captured by the Rebels, at Knoxville, tried and sentenced there, and kept at Richmond for a long time, had been executed, and urged that I be executed in retaliation.[1] This seemed to solve the mystery of my return to prison under such a strong guard, and for a few days the suspense, both to myself and my friends, was very trying indeed; more especially to my good mother, as the East Tennessee Unionists took great pleasure in telling her that I would certainly be executed.

CHAPTER 9

A few days after my return to prison, some one cried out: "Captain R. G. Clark is wanted at the gate!," and all eyes were turned upon me as I marched out of the prison to the gate. I had not the slightest idea as to what they wanted with me, and whilst I never at any time believed that they would execute me, I must confess that under the circumstances this call gave me a feeling of dreadful suspense, until the gate opened upon my approach, and Ed. Trigg, United States marshall [in Knoxville], handed me a warrant to read, charging me with treason against the United States government. [*The indictment is dated December 27, 1864.*][2] I certainly felt shaky, as it was impossible for me to know whether it was a civil process to be served on me, or a file of soldiers to march me out to be shot; and I will say frankly that it was a source of great relief to return to the jail a prisoner of the civil authorities instead of the military. The man who was executed by President Davis's order was commissioned by Andrew Johnson[3] whilst he [Johnson] was Military Governor of Tennessee, as a recruiting captain, and after being tried by [Confederate] court martial as a spy, was sentenced to be hung. When the Federals approached Knoxville [at the end of August 1863], this man, whose name I do not remember, was removed to Richmond. Why President Davis ordered him to be executed after waiting so long, and until the Confederate cause seemed almost hopeless, has been always a mystery. It certainly seemed very inopportune for me.

A short time after this the Yankee sergeant came into the prison and said: "President Lincoln has been assassinated [April 14, 1865], and you will catch h—l now!" I wondered what was to take place next.

About this time, and near the close of the war, some prisoners were brought in at night, and not recognizing those of the party whom I met, I passed to my bunk without the knowledge that some of them belonged to my own company, until some one handed me a note, which read: "Your brother John was killed at Elizabethtown [Elizabethton, Tennessee] yesterday," and signed "George Crosby."[4] Thus ended the life of a kind brother, an honest man and patriotic soldier. He was my senior by several years, and by his fatherly care and sympathy gave me great comfort in the trying experience through which we were called to pass.

There were some hardships, not to say cruelties, perpetrated upon the Union people of East Tennessee during the early part of the war. Some were carried off to prison without just cause, as I thought, and there were some bridge burners hung.[5] These seemed to me harsh measures, but I suppose the Confederate authorities regarded the matter as being one of great importance, and thought it necessary to make an example of these men. These things were held by Union people in justification of their cruelties to the Confederates after the war, when men were shot down for no other reason than that they belonged to the Confederate army. Ab Baker,[6] whose father was killed by the Union people early in the war at his home near Knoxville, came to town with his uncle one day shortly after the close of the war to attend to business connected with the father's estate. Baker, who belonged to one of the best families in the State, had surrendered with his command, come home and was peaceably pursuing his business affairs. A young man by the name of Hall,[7] a disciple of Brownlow, called the attention of some bystanders, saying they could see some fun now while he horsewhipped Baker. He crossed the street and met Baker and his uncle coming out of the court house, and let in on him; but he soon discovered, to his consternation, that Baker was pulling a pistol from his pocket, and broke to run, when Baker killed him. The officer came forward to arrest Baker, but was told to stand back, that he would surrender only on the distinct understanding that he was to be protected. This was promised, and Baker was put into the same cell [the iron cage] which I had occupied so long. The Baker family were high strung and famous for their courage and integrity. That night a mob stormed the jail, took Baker out and hung him to a tree.[8]

CHAPTER 9

Fig. 22. Knoxville County Court House, from a sketch by Theodore R. Davis. From *Harper's Weekly*, 1864, p. 232.

When the war finally ended in the spring of 1865 I was still a prisoner, charged with treason against the United States Government. It was in May, 1865, that I was carried under guard to the Federal court [fig. 22], Judge Trigg presiding, to have my case investigated on the question of being admitted to bail. [*There was no civil court in Knoxville during the war until May 17, 1864, when Judge Connelly F. Trigg convened Federal District Court.*][9] It was made a rule of the court that any one who was shown to be guilty of murder or any bad crime, should not be admitted to bail. A long and tedious investigation ensued on the charges made against me by Brownlow. [*Court records show a capias (arrest warrant) issued on March 6, 1865, and subpoenas on May 31 and June 2, 7 and 8, 1865; the subpoenas undoubtedly correspond to RGC's various court appearances.*][10] Witnesses were summoned from all parts of that section, and when one lot was exhausted, the attorney general would appeal to the court for time to procure more. Thus they kept me before the court for weeks, until my friends were worried out with suspense. The prosecuting attorney, Colonel Hall,[11] of Rogersville, Tennessee, was very bitter, and prejudiced by his partisan bias, prosecuted me to the full extent of his ability. There were a great many witnesses examined without producing a particle of testimony to sustain the charges made by Mr. Brownlow, and when my attorney began to call for prominent citizens to prove my character, instead of being a criminal, I was made to feel that in reality I was about the nicest fellow in all the country. Finally Judge Trigg said to the prosecuting attorney, Colonel Hall: "It seems to me that you have had every facility for establishing the prisoner's guilt that could be asked of the court; I have allowed you every scope, both in the interest of public justice and to give the prisoner the benefit of a thorough investigation . . ." Here Colonel Hall interrupted the Judge, saying that he had a paper to read, which was as follows: "Bob Kyle, Jr.,[12] will swear that Clark told him that he (Clark) ordered Gray killed," signed "W. G. Brownlow." John Brownlow,[13] a son of the notorious W. G. Brownlow, was sitting back watching for the effect of this boomerang; doubtless he had handed in the paper a few moments before. Col. Netherland, one of my attorneys and an uncle of young Kyle, arose at once and said to the court, "Kyle is in town, and I will have him here in a few minutes." The court waited but a short time when my counsel returned with Kyle, who was sworn and put on the witness stand. What he was going to swear I had no means of knowing, though I knew that he was of good family and a nice young man and I could not think that he would swear falsely. Col. Netherland read the document to him and asked him what he had to say touching the truth or falsity. Kyle replied that there was no truth in it; that he had not met Captain Clark since the war commenced. My counsel asked him if he knew of any conduct on the part of Clark that was dishonorable. "None whatever," replied Kyle.

It is useless to say that my pursuers did not know there was nothing in this Kyle story, for they had scoured that whole end of the State in pursuit of evidence upon which to keep me in prison. His [Hall's] point was to arrest Judge Trigg's decision to admit me to bail, seeing that the judge had made up his mind to do so. So he resorted to the subterfuge of having Kyle summoned, thinking he was at his home some sixty miles distant, thus hoping to obtain more time in which he could hatch up something else upon which he might possibly prevent my coming out of prison. This was the last witness in the case, and Judge Trigg's patience was about exhausted.[14] He turned to the clerk of court and ordered him to take my bond, which he said he had no doubt I was amply able to make. Much to my gratification a number of prominent citizens, including a portion of the bar, stepped promptly to the clerk, unsolicited by me, and signed my bond for ten thousand dollars; and for the first time in eight long and weary months I was again free [*June 8, 1865. The trial was set for January 3, 1866*].[15] Passing out of the court house with C. M. McClung, one of the best friends I ever had, I was denouncing Brownlow when he [McClung] took me by the arm and said: "Clark, hush; you will be killed before you know what you are doing. You go down to my house with my little son, Matt, and remain there until I come home."[16]

In a short time quite a number of ladies called to see me and cautioned me against going on the streets, as Confederates were being shot down without the slightest warning. Having been locked up in prison so long, I had no conception of the extent of the reign of terror under Brownlow's regime. [*For example, Brownlow's* Whig and Rebel Ventilator *for June 7, 1865, carried a strident anti-Rebel article from the* Nashville Press and Times, *especially decrying leniency for Rebel officers and leaders, "those whose social position was thought to make their persons too sacred to be imprisoned in a felon's cell. . . . Let the leaders of the rebellion terribly expatiate their atrocious offense either by exile, dungeon or scaffold."*] It was made too hot for all Confederates, and the fact was painfully evident that the Brownlow party were bent upon maltreating, robbing and driving the Confederates and their sympathizers out of the country. Some of the courts even sanctioned their nefarious schemes.

Having determined not to be driven out without availing myself of the opportunity to see friends, I remained in the city for several weeks, during which time, against the advice of friends, I walked the streets day and night at pleasure. I could hear the soldiers cursing me as I passed them, but never came in personal contact with any of them.

On one occasion my friend, John Helmes,[17] sent me word to get off the streets; that a Federal outlaw had just threatened to kill me on sight. I went down to his office and asked him for particulars, and investigated the fellow, of whom I had never had any knowledge, and from all the information I could get, concluded that it was the empty threat of some low down, arrant coward, and paid no further attention to it. I was heavily armed all the time, and determined to sell out as dearly as possible in case I was attacked.

Finally I left Knoxville for Virginia; stopped at Bristol [Tennessee] for several weeks and then went to Lynchburg, where I remained about two months. At Lynchburg I found a lot of tobacco that had been purchased by Clark & Mayo during the early part of the war and stored there. The gentleman, Mr. Taylor,[18] who had it in charge, told me that it would bring but little more than enough to pay the taxes on it. Being much in need of funds, I instructed him to sell it for what it would bring. On that day I went to Bedford County [Virginia] to wait on Captain Slicer, who married a Miss Williams,[19] and upon my return to Lynchburg Mr. Taylor handed me an account of sales of the tobacco and $3,300 which it netted me.

I then went to Washington to obtain a special pardon from President Johnson,[20] and having succeeded [October 26, 1865], went to the next term of the Federal court at Knoxville, presented my pardon and was fully discharged.[21] [*In RGC's first petition for pardon, written in his own hand, he states that*

> he is deprived of the benefits of the amnesty oath provided by the late Proclamation on account of an indictment for treason lately found in the Fed-

eral Court at Knoxville, but is not included within any other accepted class: that he was originally a Union man and opposed to secession at the commencement of the Rebellion, that he has taken the oath of [allegiance] . . . and now wishes and prays to be allowed to return to this allegiance to the constitution of the United States and the union of the States thereunder.

Two formal versions of the petition, one dated September 28, the other undated and in a flourished chancery hand, omit the mention of RGC's pre-war Union sympathies. Most likely there were enough petitioners declaring similar loyalties as to make all such claims suspect. Letters of recommendation of RGC were signed variously by John Williams, G. M. Hazen, W. C. Kyle, John M. Fleming, Alvin Barton, James H. Cowan, Perez Dickinson, R. A. Crawford, John Baxter, James C. Luttrell, and William Heiskell. Cowan and Dickinson had been RGC's pre-war employers, Judge John Baxter was one of his defense attorneys, and Heiskell the Commissioner of the Circuit Court of East Tennessee who certified RGC's amnesty oath on June 19. In a note from Nashville, dated October 25, then Governor William G. Brownlow wrote the U.S. Attorney General, "I decline recommending the pardon of Mr. Clark"; at least Brownlow cannot be accused of hypocrisy. A treason trial was nevertheless held on December 18, 1865. RGC requested a jury, which acquitted him, and after paying thirty dollars in court fees, he was again discharged.][22] For a time after this I was a wanderer. I first went to Memphis, Tennessee, but could get nothing to do there. I then went to Arkansas and entered into a partnership with a planter to raise cotton. Cotton was then worth forty five to fifty cents per pound. Having invested what limited means I could command in this enterprise, I discovered before the crop matured that the planter with whom I had made the engagement was badly involved, and I had considerable trouble in getting my money back.

Disgusted with my experience in this venture, I returned to Georgia and stopped at Atlanta for two months, going from there to Mont Vale Springs, near Knoxville; on the way I stopped over at Rome, Georgia, with a view to making it my home. I met a number of people in Rome, to whom I was introduced by Mr. Thomas Berry.[23] Among those to whom I was introduced was Mr. Peter Hardin, who said to me that he would be glad if I would buy out his partner, Mr. Johnson,[24] and engage in business with him, as Mr. Johnson did not stay in Rome.

I wrote to Johnson on the subject, and asked him to meet me at Mont Vale Springs. Not very long afterward I was at Mont Vale Springs, and while on the ballroom floor dancing the "lancers" with Miss Pollard,[25] of Montgomery, one night, some one informed me that a gentleman on the veranda wished to speak to me. As soon as I could excuse myself I went out and found that it was Mr. Johnson who wished to see me. I bought his interest in the business of Hardin & Johnson, and thus became a fixture in Rome.

Rome, Ga.,
November, 1891.

Epilogue

Reuben Grove Clark did indeed become a fixture in Rome, Georgia. He remained there for the rest of his life, had considerable success in business, and became one of the most respected members of the community. Like many Civil War officers, he was addressed throughout his life by his military rank, as Captain Clark.

On September 8, 1868, when he was thirty-five, Reuben married Susan Alice Smith (1847–1891), daughter of Asahel R. Smith, a citizen of Rome with roots in Vermont; they had two daughters.[1] He was still a lively, handsome man when left a widower at age fifty-eight, and it is not surprising that a friend of his now grown daughters found him attractive (fig. 23). Mary Josephine ("Daisy") King (1857–1936) of Savannah, was the daughter of the Reverend Charles Barrington King and Anna Wylly Habersham King (fig. 24).[2] She and Reuben were married January 9, 1894, and of this union three children were born.[3] Members of the family belonged to the First Presbyterian Church in Rome.[4]

Soon after settling in Rome, Reuben established a retail business with Peter H. Hardin. In 1873 he was junior partner in the founding of a firm known as McWilliams & Co. The name was changed in 1885 to R. G. Clark & Co., with A. W. Tedcastle, an Englishman and company employee, as junior partner. Under both names the store occupied a large three-story brick building in downtown Rome and sold wholesale dry goods, including notions, shoes, and hats, through-

Fig. 23. Reuben G. Clark, about 1894.

Fig. 24. Mary Josephine ("Daisy") King Clark, about 1894.

out north Georgia.⁵ Clark became a civic leader and was also active in local banking as president of the Merchants National Bank. With typical late Victorian flourishes, the *Rome City Directory* of 1888 summarized his achievements:

Captain Reuben Grove Clark

Among the most prominent and active citizens of Rome, no one stands higher or is more generally respected than the subject of this sketch.

Capt. Clark is a native of East Tennessee, and in rugged honesty and stability of character he may be happily likened to the great, solidly fastened mountains under whose shadows he was born. [*There follows a brief account of his childhood, youth and military service.*]

After the [Civil War] was over . . . Captain Clark took up the broken threads of the life of a citizen, and in this city began anew the contest for the honors and successes which come in some measure to all honest toilers in the world of commerce. With but a small capital, a partnership was formed with P. H. Hardin and a retail store was opened. Diligence, strictest integrity, keen judgment, courtesy; these were the characteristics of the firm, and in a short while success was assured. From the smallest beginning has been developed a magnificent business, and now the firm is one of the largest and strongest in the State, with a standing in the commercial ranks which may be called "gilt-edged," and employs a capital of more than a half million dollars. Captain Clark is also president of the Merchants Bank, and as such has shown consummate ability as a financier.

In his social and domestic life, as a public-spirited citizen, as a Christian gentleman, Captain Clark is honored, loved, looked up to and spotless. He is true to his convictions, charitable, helpful to the worthy struggling, and brave in standing by the right. No Roman stands higher than this one.⁶

Reuben Clark continued to be interested in state and national politics, now as an economic Liberal and Gold Democrat. After Grover

Fig. 25. "Belle Vue," the Clark home in Rome, Georgia. Photograph courtesy of the Savannah Historical Society.

Cleveland's defeat in the 1888 presidential election, Clark wrote to Daniel S. Lamont, Cleveland's long-time friend and advisor, to express his dismay. Cleveland had shown in his first term that he was an honest man of tough moral fiber in both domestic and foreign affairs, and a champion of entrepreneurs and farmers, qualities that appealed to Reuben, as his letter shows:

> Rome, Ga., Nov. 13, 1888.
> Col. Daniel S. Lamont,
> Washington DC
>
> Dear Sir
>
> Though a stranger I beg to express through you to the President my deep sense of mortification and disappointment at the defeat of the best Executive the Country has ever had, and also the hope that his manly patriotic and statesmanlike Administration in the interest of the people will be fully vindicated four years hence in his triumphant Election to the Presidency in 1892. I was in New York Election day and honestly believe the Election was bought.[7] Mr. Cleveland has fully met every responsibility in his high office patriotically and will I believe remain the leader of his party untill they again call him to the White House.
>
> With great admiration for the President as well as for the Lady who has illustrated above others, beautiful propriety under all circumstances.
>
> I subscribe myself an humble Citizen of Georgia.
>
> > Yours truly
> > R. G. Clark[8]

Despite Cleveland's difficult and largely unsuccessful second term, 1893–97, Reuben's loyalty did not falter. At Christmas-time 1896 he sent a locally raised turkey as a gift to the president.[9] Family lore notes that the bird was an extremely big one.

In 1880, after having lived near the center of town, Clark purchased seventeen acres in suburban East Rome and built a large frame house, called "Belle Vue," designed in the "bracketed Italian" manner (fig. 25). The family lived stylishly. Their coachman, a black man named Aaron Dent, hardly over four feet tall, looked imposing when he mounted "the coachman's box of the Clark landau, and, whipping up his two horses, drove Miss Carrie and Miss Rosa Clark to town."[10] Old glass negatives show Reuben and his second wife Daisy and her children on the lawn of the home and in the landau.[11] He and Daisy made at least one visit to Knoxville.[12] This may have been in 1897 when Daisy and her first two children went for a stay at Old Sweet Springs, West Virginia, to be followed soon by the captain. A letter from Reuben to Daisy at this time reveals the warmth he felt for his family and his concern with domestic matters, perhaps a bit unusual for a Victorian gentleman.

Aug. 20, 1897

Bank Office of R. G. Clark
My dear wife

I send package by Express to day for the darling babies and Will[13] marked names on them. As you will see Josephine gets the lion's share. Told Will I would like to send you something but didn't know what to send. He said Daisy likes cash. She always did like cash. So if you need money call on Mr White untill I come. I left some money with him. I do wish so much that you could have some of the great abundance of the nice fruit here. Water mellons & cantelopes have both sold as loss at 50¢ for wagon load. Never saw anything like it and the finest quality I ever saw. Peaches same way. Am putting up some plums or rather Carrie is having it done. We will have pies next summer. Park & Tilford say the box milk will be sent at once.

I sent off the curtains this morning by freight as they made a large heavy package. The Gentleman from Atlanta who is cleaning our carpets seems to be a nice man. He has moved to East Rome and is a Presbyterian—has cleaned the Parks carpet and it looks like a new carpet. He says the idea of taking up that carpet is ridiculous so I will buy new carpet for the dining room and let that remain. I do hope he can clean the other carpets as nicely especially the ones above and below in family part of the house. About the general cleaning up we are going to do as you suggested—let the servants do it after we leave. Have told them that we don't want to see a speck of dirt inside the house when we get home.

I plucked those roses with my own hands off the bed below the drive way. Paul Cooper[14] goes to NY with me on 2^d and I would like to get to the Springs by the 12th if possible but it may be 15th. With a great deal of love and kisses for the Chicks

Reuben[15]

This contented life came to an end for Reuben Grove Clark on March 28, 1900, when, after being chilled in a rainy sports outing, he contracted pneumonia and died. It was a quiet death for a man who led a robust life, faced danger courageously, overcame intense physical suffering, and succeeded in virtually every endeavor. He added still more luster to that life by leaving an interesting and informative account of his part in some of the most important historical events of his region and his nation.

Appendix

The Fifty-ninth Tennessee Mounted Infantry and Company I

Only one history of the Fifty-ninth Tennessee has been written, the account in *Tennesseans in the Civil War*.[1] While this remarkable work records all Tennessee military units and most of the servicemen, Confederate and Union, who enlisted from Tennessee, its regimental histories are relatively short and are undocumented. As a consequence of the new information on the Fifty-ninth provided by Reuben Clark, I have undertaken to expand the regiment's history and to document that history as fully as I am able.

Sometime around February 17, 1862, five independent East Tennessee volunteer military companies were united to form the First Battalion of Tennessee Infantry under Major William L. Eakin, in the command of Brigadier General Edmund Kirby Smith.[2] Although the original five are not specified in the Compiled Service Records, the seven companies that were eventually incorporated into the battalion include the following: James Burch Cooke's (later Company A), J. P. Brown's (later Company B), James Brook's (later Company C), Henry D. Geisler's (later Company F), Josiah I. Wright's (later Company G), John B. Cobb's (later Company H), and William H. Smith's (later Company I). With the addition, about May 1862, of troops that became E and K Companies, also from East Tennessee, the unit reached regimental strength. The first Conscript Act, of April 16, 1862, brought sudden increases in both forced and volunteer enlistments, and occasioned the reorganization of the army, including local volunteer units.[3] It was in this context that on June 30, 1862, eleven Tennessee companies together were designated the Fifty-ninth Tennessee Infantry (also known as Cooke's regiment, later Eakin's) of the Confederate Army. Not until November 1863, after the regiment had joined the brigade of Brigadier General John C. Vaughn, was it mounted. The first regimental commander was James Burch Cooke, who captained one of the original companies and who was elected colonel in the new unit;[4] Major Eakin was second in command. The other regimental officers were Major Charles M. Alexander, replaced by Major (then Lieutenant Colonel) James P. Brown; Major James F. Love; Major Henry D. Geisler; W. D. Van Dyke, commissary; W. T. Russell and Samuel Strick, chaplains. Cumulatively for the period of the war there were eighteen captains, including Reuben G. Clark.[5]

Company I was organized at Bean Station, Tennessee in the Fall of 1861. The officers elected included William H. Smith as captain, Reuben G. Clark as first lieutenant, John B. Shields and Thomas Stolsworth as second lieutenants; as first sergeant Reese Ore, and as second sergeant William H. Long. Later in the war Shields became first lieutenant and then captain, William H. Long and Samuel H. Hickle second lieutenants.[6] Shields's reminiscences of the war, cited here in a number of instances, both extend and confirm Reuben Clark's account. The company was ordered to report to Captain Cooke, then in the First Battalion of Tennessee Volunteers at Bethel Spring, near Morristown, and designated Company I.[7]

Shortly thereafter all or part of the battalion was sent to Knoxville where it encamped at Flint Hill until June 22, 1862. The men drilled regularly and provided guards for the city and on passenger trains in and out of Knoxville.[8] It was during this period in Knoxville, when it was in Confederate hands, that men from what would be the Fifty-ninth Tennessee Infantry regiment figured in the history of the contentious William G. Brownlow, Knoxville publisher and fanatical Unionist, who would later bedevil Reuben Clark during his sojourn in the Union military prison in Knoxville, and even after the peace came. From sometime in January until February 16, 1862, men from Company A, still apparently commanded by Burch Cooke, were in charge of the Knoxville jail. They were ordered to guard the residence in which Brownlow was held under house arrest for fostering bridge burning.[9] In the fullness of his anger, indignation, and paranoia, Brownlow reviled the guarding troops, calling them profane, ill-mannered, and drunkards.[10] When Cooke was captured in August 1864, Brownlow, now publishing in a Federally controlled Knoxville, reported the capture with particular glee, calling Cooke "one of the most unmitigated scoundrels in the rebel ranks."[11] It would have been consistent with Brownlow's character that the experience with Cooke in 1862 encouraged the "Parson" to avenge himself later on Clark, as a member of Cooke's regiment.

After its formation in June 1862, and for the remainder of the year, the Fifty-ninth Tennessee was an unattached infantry regiment, associated with one or another brigade in Kirby Smith's Department of East Tennessee. A troop list of June 30 notes the Fifty-ninth as unattached, and on July 3 as with Colonel T. H. Taylor's Fifth Brigade in Brigadier General Carter L. Stevenson's First Division.[12] A list of October 31, 1862, has the regiment still unattached, but serving in the Fourth Brigade of Colonel Alexander W. Reynolds, where it would be brigaded early in 1863.[13]

On June 22, 1862, shortly before they officially became the Fifty-ninth Tennessee, all companies of the regiment were ordered to Strawberry Plains, Tennessee, just east of Knoxville, under the command of now Lieutenant Colonel Eakin; they remained in the area through most of the summer.[14] There is no record of Colonel Cooke's whereabouts during this period, but he was again in command on the July 3 troop list. On the day the regiment was officially formed it was temporarily divided, two companies being recorded with the Second Brigade.[15] The overall mission in the region was to quell Unionists' attempts to disrupt communications, for on July 1 Colonel Eakin received a letter warning him of Federal soldiers and of "spies and guides" conspiring to burn bridges at Strawberry Plains and Loudon.[16]

Late in the summer and into the fall, between August 18 and October 16, Company I was on duty at Noes Ferry, Tennessee, guarding against bushwhackers.[17] Meanwhile, on August 23, two unspecified companies of the Fifty-ninth were sent to Morristown, Tennessee, to report to General Stevenson. The order noted that four companies, with the headquarters, were already at Strawberry Plains, one at Flat Creek and three at Knoxville.[18] On August 25, 1862, Colonel Cooke was ordered to report at once to General Stevenson, and although not so indicated on the order, preparations were being made to send the Fifty-ninth on a campaign with Major General Braxton Bragg and Brigadier General Kirby Smith to bring Kentucky into the Confederacy. The entire group from the Fifty-ninth was allowed only five wagons, and each company one tent; all else was to go by rail or to be put in storage; each man would receive three days' rations and forty rounds of ammunition.[19] Why Company I was left behind in Tennessee is not known. Stevenson's division, which included the troops from the Fifty-ninth Tennessee, was led by Kirby Smith and took part in the Confederate victory at Richmond, Kentucky (August 30), that opened the way to Lexington. The division was present in Frankfort when Bragg and Kirby Smith installed a Confederate governor, Richard C. Hawes, an event that did not, however, carry Kentucky into the Confederacy. The battle of Perryville was still ahead, and it would not end happily for the Confederate armies. Bragg anticipated a fight near Lexington and ordered Kirby Smith to take his forces to that area. When the fighting began to the south in Perryville on October 8, Kirby Smith's troops were too far away to be of help and arrived too late for the battle. Outnumbered more than two to one and considering a victory beyond their grasp, the Confederates withdrew after that first day of battle and headed back to Tennessee.[20]

On October 16, 1862, Company I proceeded to Tazewell, Tennessee, to rejoin its regiment retreating out of Kentucky.[21] After that the Fifty-ninth was encamped in winter quarters at Lenoir City, Tennessee, little knowing that they would soon be called to one of the decisive campaigns of the war.[22] Company I's history now appears to follow that of the whole regiment, except where Reuben Clark mentions special brief assignments, such as his occupation of Martinsburg in 1864. The regiment was still in Stevenson's division when on December 18 orders came for that unit to report to Major General John C. Pemberton at Vicksburg.[23] Here at last, in the Department of Mississippi and East Louisiana, the Fifty-ninth Tennessee was brigaded as part of the defense force guarding the all-important gateway to the upper Mississippi. It was on January 31, 1863, that the regiment became part of Colonel Reynolds's Fourth Brigade (Stevenson's Division), with which it remained and fought in the long, bloody, and demoralizing Vicksburg campaign.[24] The brigade was large, with 183 officers and 2,422 men, but its numbers were reduced to 163 officers and 1,950 men after the battles of Port Gibson and Champion Hill later in the spring of that year.[25] Colonel (later Brigadier General) Reynolds (1816–76; fig. 7), a Virginian and West Point graduate, was the only one of the Fifty-ninth's three principal higher commanders (the other two were Vaughn and Breckinridge) who was a trained professional soldier.[26]

Upon arrival at Vicksburg on December 29, 1862, the Fifty-ninth was ordered, as Clark notes, to proceed immediately to relieve Stevenson at the battle of Chickasaw Bluff. Because of the dark, the extremely difficult terrain, and a torrential rain, the regiment did not arrive until daylight, by which time the battle was over and the Federals defeated. For failing to comply with orders, the regimental commander, Colonel Cooke, was arrested, probably on December 30. He was court-martialed, but when details of the regiment's ordeal in the dark swamps became known, he was acquitted. Nonetheless, because of chronic diarrhea, one of the most prevalent conditions in both armies, and liver disease, he resigned soon after from the service;[27] he rejoined later, only to be captured in August 1864.[28] Colonel Eakin, who had commanded the regiment at Strawberry Plain, was given permanent command.

By January 25, 1863, the Fifty-ninth was in defensive positions at Warrenton, Mississippi, below Vicksburg.[29] The winter saw no major encounters, but there was much skirmishing and a continuing bombardment. The pace was considerably quickened on April 29, 1863, as Reuben states, when the regiment was put on a forced march to reinforce Brigadier General Edward D. Tracy at Port Gibson, where Federal troops under then Brigadier General Ulysses S. Grant were about to begin their successful second push toward Vicksburg. As a result of some apparent confusion in orders, or possibly in geographic orientation, Reynolds's brigade did not arrive as expected at a defensive location at Grindstone Ford, near Bayou Pierre, which caused consternation at headquarters, but evidently no significant repercussions for either Reynolds or the brigade.[30] Outnumbered five to one, the Confederates were overwhelmed and during the night—Reuben says about 2 A.M.—were ordered back to Vicksburg.

The next battle in which the Fifty-ninth took part was one of the most important actions of the war. On Friday, May 15, Stevenson's division left Vicksburg about 5 P.M. at the rear of Pemberton's army on its way east in the rain to meet Grant in what is known as the battle of Champion Hill (or Baker's Creek), May 16, 1863. The division halted for the night on the Raymond Road, and about 8 A.M. the next day Reynolds's brigade was assigned to turn the supply train of some 400 wagons around to become the van of a movement toward Brownsville, following General Joseph E. Johnston's orders to Pemberton to join him north of the Southern Railroad between Vicksburg and Jackson.[31] The brigade was further ordered to guard the trains. Reynolds turned the wagons and deployed one detachment in front, a regiment on the right flank, and the rest of the infantry and artillery to the rear of the advancing train. His troops saw action in skirmishes until about 3 P.M., by which time Confederate forces were badly beaten and in retreat. Reynolds was ordered to withdraw part of his forces across the Big Black River to Vicksburg and, with the rest, to go to the aid of Brigadier General Seth M. Barton at the Jackson Road Bridge. A Union force had meanwhile taken over the bridge as Barton retreated, and Reynolds, seeing the enemy moving to cut him off, veered from the road. In a shrewd maneuver to elude detection, he marched his men through the woods parallel to the enemy advance and was able eventually to rejoin his command.[32] Around 3 o'clock in the morning of May 17, Reynolds's troops crossed the Big Black on a pontoon bridge at Bridgeport. They remained at Bridgeport, destroying the boats there, then went to Bovina where they were ordered to continue on to Vicksburg. By about 5 P.M. on the 17th the brigade was back in the beleaguered city with the supply trains.[33]

The Confederate retreat had been difficult, but Reynolds could praise his troops for performing well in "the arduous marches and perilous positions" they had had to endure.[34] By contrast, Pemberton, describing the defeat to President Davis, stated that "many regiments behaved badly."[35] Stevenson, the division commander, was censured for not having maintained his position a sufficiently long time. Yet he was moved to commend Reynolds for performing his guard duties with efficiency and fidelity.[36] In a memo of that day Pemberton too commended Reynolds's "judicious management" in that operation.[37] Although the brigade was not in the thick of things at Champion Hill, during the Confederate retreat a number of the Fifty-ninth's men were killed during the action known as the battle of the Big Black, but the regiment's greatest losses were to capture.[38] The Confederate defeat at Champion Hill was more than a prelude to the ultimate fall of Vicksburg: Champion Hill is considered the turning point of the Mississippi campaign, if not of the entire war.[39]

The siege of Vicksburg began on May 18. The Fifty-ninth Tennessee, with other Tennessee units, had been sent to the ditches below the city and assigned to a position between Barton's First Brigade and Brigadier General Alfred Cumming's Third Brigade.[40] According to Reuben Clark, his regiment was deployed near artillery installations. On maps of the Vicksburg defenses Stevenson's entire division is shown arrayed on the long heights overlooking the river to the south of the city, with Reynolds's brigade on the far left (fig. 8).[41] The performance of some of Stevenson's brigades at Champion Hill had been weak, and Pemberton felt that this location would be, initially at least, less challenging than some others.[42] Yet these perimeter defenses were not without strategic importance, and the men of the Fifty-ninth and others in the trenches stayed in their positions for the entire seven weeks of the siege, under almost constant bombardment from batteries on land and on Union vessels in the river. As Colonel Reynolds remarked, his troops were, "often half-fed and illy-clothed," but they remained "constant and courageous" until the surrender of the city on July 4, 1863.[43] An early chronicler of the Confederate military stated that during the siege of Vicksburg the Third, Thirty-ninth, and Fifty-ninth Tennessee Regiments "were conspicuous for their valour and endurance."[44] Reuben describes briefly but poignantly the pitiful condition of his starved compatriots at the time of surrender. Another Confederate wrote, "We were short of provisions, so that our men . . . had eaten mule meat and rats and young shoots of cane. . . . We were so short-handed that no man within the lines had ever been off duty more than a small part of each day," and all were "exhausted and unfit for any duty but simply standing in the trenches and firing."[45] When Pemberton capitulated, Confederate forces had been on reduced rations for some time and had only a week's supply left, at the reduced rate.[46]

More than 29,000 Confederate troops surrendered at Vicksburg on the symbolically charged day of July 4. Weapons were stacked on the 5th, and that evening General Grant, dressed as usual like a common soldier, rode around near the Confederate breastworks where members of the Fifty-ninth Tennessee saw him at close range.[47] The surviving members of the regiment were paroled during the following week, most on July 10. The Record of Events for Company F for June–October 1863, states that after being paroled, the men marched 150 miles to Enterprise, Mississippi, and from there they left for their homes in East Tennessee.[48] In behavior common to most Confederate units, some of the men never returned to the regiment, and some defected to the Union army with a promise of protection.[49] The troops of the Fifty-ninth were officially exchanged on September 12,[50] and thereafter mounted;[51] some were assigned to duty as scouts and guides for Brigadier General John S. Williams, commander of Confederate troops east of Knoxville.[52] Reuben Clark puts parts of the regiment at Dalton, Georgia, a rail center and major encampment site, just after the battle of Chickamauga (September 19, 1863).[53]

It was at Dalton, on October 11, that the first commander of Company I, Captain William H. Smith, submitted his resignation from military service, and probably here that Reuben was made a captain on October 17. Smith had begun showing symptoms of tuberculosis in the Fall of 1862,[54] and the hardships of Vicksburg must have accelerated the illness's progress, for by January 31, 1863, Reuben Clark had succeeded Smith as company commander.[55]

Reynolds's brigade was combined by November 6, 1863, with that of Brigadier General John C. Vaughn, who in 1861 had commanded Reuben Clark's first regiment, the Third Tennessee. Vaughn was put in command of the new brigade, which was then ordered to take a position at Sweet Water, Tennessee.[56] The Fifty-ninth Tennessee Regiment remained in Vaughn's brigade for the rest of the war.

General Vaughn (1824–75) was born in Roane City, Tennessee (fig. 11). He joined the U.S. Army for a time and saw action in the Mexican War. Upon returning to Tennessee he established a retail business. When secession came, he sided with the Confederacy and on May 29, 1861, in Knoxville, he organized the Third Tennessee

Infantry Regiment and was elected its commanding colonel; he became a brigadier on September 22, 1862. Although Vaughn's superiors considered his military skills, including troop discipline, modest or even lax, he was a brave and dedicated Confederate commander. In February 1865, with his troops in rags and low in provisions, arms, and ammunition, Vaughn wrote to his commander in the Department of Southwest Virginia, Brigadier General John Echols, that although he was not a West Pointer (neither was Echols), he would obey orders and "my heart is in this death struggle of ours and I want to do my duty."[57] He was liked and respected, but not revered, by his men. Near the war's end, fighting a holding campaign on his home territory, Vaughn was to demonstrate a tenacity and a prowess in battle that would at last earn him praise as a commander.[58]

On October 23, 1863, Vaughn indicated that the Vicksburg defeat was still having adverse repercussions on the brigade. From Sweet Water, he wrote to President Davis to express his consternation that the Vicksburg parolees in East Tennessee were not reporting for duty. He also stated that his brigade had still not been officially exchanged, which cannot refer to the entire brigade, for as noted, the Fifty-ninth Tennessee had been exchanged in September. He requests authority to turn "the true men" of his three regiments, together with his own Third Tennessee, into a brigade of mounted infantry.[59] Permission to mount the brigade did not come through until about December 26, 1863, when Lieutenant General James Longstreet mentioned the fact in a letter to Adjutant General Samuel Cooper and grumped that there was already enough cavalry running about foraging off and destroying farms. Longstreet could have added, moreover, that some of the regular cavalry held mounted infantry in disdain.[60]

Late in the Fall of 1863, one or more companies of the Fifty-ninth were sent off on special assignments. Clark notes that Company I was put in charge of Athens, Tennessee, and after several weeks there joined "the line of battle" to fight in Loudon, Tennessee (probably December 4–5, 1863.)[61] Then Company I (and probably other units of the regiment) crossed on pontoon bridges to join Longstreet and the rest of the brigade lifting the siege at Knoxville on December 5, after Longstreet's unsuccessful assault on Fort Sanders on November 29. Vaughn's brigade is now listed in the Department of East Tennessee under Longstreet.[62]

On December 31, 1863, the Fifty-ninth Tennessee had a new, although temporary, commander, Lieutenant Colonel James P. Brown of Company B.[63] No reason for the change has been found, but it may have been that Eakin was ill, an all too common problem in both armies. By January 31, 1864, Colonel Eakin had returned to the Fifty-ninth and was still regimental commander on March 31.[64]

By late 1863 Confederate forces, from the start less numerous than those of the North, were disastrously depleted from battle casualties, as well as from the usual illnesses and desertions. Recombinations of units occurred at an increasing pace. On January 31, 1864, Vaughn's brigade was attached to Major General William T. Martin's cavalry corps.[65] In the Fifty-ninth the difficulties of mounting and especially of reassembling a scattered regiment were still vexing its commander as late as February. The problems are outlined in a letter Eakin wrote to Vaughn:

> Hd Qrs 59th Regt Tenn Vols.
> Near Rogersville Tenn,
> Febry 7th 1864.
> Brig. Gen Jno C. Vaughn.

Sir

I would respectfully state, that a portion of my Regt, consisting mostly of men from Cos. (C & F) were seperated from the remainder of the Regiment, when Knoxville Tenn. was occupied by the enemy & are now at Dalton Geo. doing duty in the "Camp of Disections." These men had been mounted and did duty for a time, in uper East Tenn, in Gen. [Robert] Ransom's command but were dismounted and sent round for the purpose of joining their command, but left their horses in Sulivan County Tenn, the place of their homes. Now since the remainder of the Regt is with Gen. Longstreet and your Brigade has been ordered to be mounted, it is important that these men return to their Regiment when they can[;] *all*, as I am informed, mounted themselves. I would ask, if it is not incompatable with the best interest of the service, that you procure an order from the Honorable Secretary of War directing them to be sent round to their command at the earliest possible day. I need scarcely add that it is difficult to render a portion or portions of Regiments efficient when they are divided as mine now is.[66]

The Muster Roll of Company F for January through February 1864 shows it was still at Dalton, Georgia, but notes that the company started off by the southern route to join the regiment in Rogersville, Tennessee, by order of General Johnston. Other units were gathered in only slowly, the men staying home probably to chop wood and care for their families in the cold of a Tennessee mountain winter. The brigade had gone into winter quarters on Big Creek near Rogersville, and Vaughn's command, still with a mere four hundred to five hundred effectives, partly mounted, moved about in the northernmost mountains on defense or intelligence missions at Tazewell, Bean Station, Cumberland Gap, Bull's Gap, Kingsport, Blountsville, and Bristol.[67] Reuben Clark reports that there was occasional skirmishing. Some of the officers, including Clark, took the opportunity to recruit in the area.[68]

General Longstreet continued to rearrange his forces, and on March 31, 1864, Vaughn is shown in command of a division, which included his brigade, in the cavalry corps commanded by Major General Robert Ransom, Jr. Sometime between April 16 and 29, the Fifty-ninth Tennessee was in western North Carolina trying to procure horses, undoubtedly to complete the mounting of Vaughn's troops.[69] Yet, with the acquisition of more horses came another problem: forage had become extremely scarce in the Tennessee mountains, and Ransom had to spread his troops from Big Sandy, Kentucky, to near Asheville, North Carolina, so that they might find food for their horses.[70]

Early summer brought renewed serious fighting, and the Fifty-ninth Tennessee and Vaughn's brigade entered upon their hardest and most continuous actions of the war, the long second Shenandoah Valley campaign, which lasted from mid-June 1864 to March 1865. In the Shenandoah the Fifty-ninth Tennessee saw more combat than at any other time. In 1862 the regiment's fighting had been mostly in skirmishes in East Tennessee, and a single minor battle on the Kentucky campaign. Then, at Vicksburg the men of the Fifty-ninth spent most of their time, apart from the battles of Port Gibson and Champion Hill, waiting and dodging artillery shells and sharpshooters' bullets. Even at Champion Hill their fighting amounted to no more than skirmishes and limited engagements. But in the Valley of Virginia the regiment took part in most of the major battles and operations: Piedmont, Lynchburg, the raid on Washington, Second Kernstown, Third Winchester, and Fisher's Hill, as well as numerous engagements and skirmishes in northern Virginia, West Virginia, and Maryland.

As Reuben Clark states, on June 4, 1864, the brigade was ordered to report to Staunton, Virginia, to join cavalry units under Brigadier General John D. Imboden and Brigadier General W. E. "Grumble" Jones, who were preparing to meet a Union army under Major General David Hunter at Piedmont. Because he was the most senior general officer, Jones was put in command of the Confederate forces.[71] Although Vaughn advised against engaging the enemy with so small a force, the battle took place the next day.[72] Clark's account of the action implies that the men of the Fifty-ninth were temporarily dismounted during this battle. The regiment does not appear in the official records of Piedmont, but regimental muster rolls confirm its presence by showing a large number of the Fifty-ninth's men captured there.[73] The brigade was deployed on the far right, but, as Clark describes the action, sometime during the earlier stages of the fighting, the Fifty-ninth was sent to the far left, traversing the full length of the battle line under heavy fire. In his report of the battle, General Hunter stated that at 1:30 in the afternoon the enemy was "massing his force on our right," the Confederate left.[74] This statement may well pinpoint the time of the Fifty-ninth's unexplained and unfortunate movement to the left. The regiment's losses were severe in killed, wounded, and captured, and among the last was Colonel Eakin, the regimental commander.[75] It would appear that sheer folly ordered a regiment to cross the entire length of the battle line under severe fire. There may, however, have been communication problems between Jones and his cavalry on the right at this moment, as well as in the well-known instance later, when Vaughn and Imboden withheld the order to fire as Union troops under Brigadier General George Crook descended on them from a nearby hill.[76] An editorial comment on Clark's memoir suggests that the Fifty-ninth's move to the left explains a gap that occurred in Confederate defenses and gave an important advantage to the Union attackers.[77] The battle ended in a resounding Confederate defeat in which the overall commander, General Jones, was killed.

General Vaughn's chagrin over the actions at Piedmont are perhaps reflected in the extreme brevity of his reports of the battle.[78] With Jones's death, command of the collected forces devolved on Vaughn, who gathered what was left of his diminished army and fell back to New Hope, Fishersville, and finally Rockfish Gap in the Blue Ridge, a rail center where the Confederates could be resupplied.[79] On June 6, the dashing Major General John C. Breckinridge (1821–75) of Kentucky was given command of what was left of Vaughn's forces (fig. 12). Breckinridge was a lawyer by training and had served the United States as a congressman, as vice-president, and as a senator. In 1860 he was the presidential candidate of the Southern Democrats. He joined the Confederacy in 1861 and became one of its ablest commanders.[80] To the dispirited survivors of Piedmont he brought skilled, imaginative, and inspiring military leadership.

Meanwhile Vaughn struggled to keep his troops in some semblance of fighting condition. He was near Charlottesville on June 8 when he wrote to Breckinridge that the enemy was closing and that his troops were low on such essentials as artillery, muskets, and ammunition.[81] Even so, on that same day several units of Vaughn's brigade were sent out to harass the Federals near Rockfish Gap. On the 9th, Breckinridge reorganized all forces in the command by dividing the infantry into two divisions, the one under Major General John A. Wharton, the other under Vaughn, whose brigade was dismounted; the cavalry was given to Imboden.[82]

To the Confederacy in the early summer of 1864, the Piedmont defeat was serious, for the Shenandoah was second in importance to Richmond itself, the great valley being the main source of foodstuffs for what was left of the Confederate armies. To defend this vital land against increasing Federal concentration in the region and to draw Federal troops away from Petersburg and Richmond, General Robert E. Lee chose as overall Valley commander Lieutenant General Jubal Anderson Early (1816–94), one of the South's most talented but controversial generals (fig. 13). A Virginia aristocrat educated at West Point, Early served for a time in the U.S. Army, then entered civilian life to become a lawyer. Although opposed to secession, he joined the Confederate forces and rose quickly to brigade and finally army command. Yet he was hardly a model of Southern gentility: he has been described as a "grizzled and profane bachelor" with a hot temper and acerbic tongue whose "falsetto country drawl constantly irritated more gentrified staffers."[83] One Confederate soldier remembered his "high-pitched drawling voice" taunting a chaplain for not fighting.[84] His dress in the field was irregular and slovenly, perhaps catering to his painful chronic arthritis, and it was widely believed that the canteen on his belt contained bourbon whiskey.[85] Early often bickered with fellow officers, both subordinates and superiors, but he was popular with his troops, who enjoyed his eccentricities and admired his bravery and military skill.[86] The Fifty-ninth Tennessee would soon be in Early's army, to remain there until the last few weeks of the war.

General Breckinridge heard that Hunter had taken Lexington and burned the Virginia Military Institute, and anticipating a Union move against the hospital and rail center of Lynchburg, the Kentuckian led his Piedmont survivors on an arduous march, June 12–16, south from Rockfish Gap along the Blue Ridge crest to fortify the city before Hunter could arrive.[87] Still recovering from an injury caused when his horse was killed beneath him at the second battle of Cold Harbor (June 1–3),[88] Breckinridge was near collapse on reaching Lynchburg. He therefore ordered Vaughn to take command, to confer on defense strategies with General D. H. Hill, who happened to be in Lynchburg, and then to place his forces on the hills around the city.[89] The order was written at 5:30 P.M. on June 16, and at 10:30 that night Vaughn had still not conferred with Hill, which caused Breckinridge much concern.[90] When General Early arrived on the scene to take overall command he made clear his lack of confidence in Vaughn, at that time the senior brigadier, by telegraphing Richmond to find a replacement for him.[91] Major General Arnold Elzey arrived to take command of Breckinridge's dismounted troops, and Major General Robert Ransom, Jr., the cavalry.[92] Vaughn was reduced to brigade command. There is no report on how Vaughn's demotion affected his troops, but it cannot have helped morale among his tired and discouraged men.

Meanwhile, earth works were hastily constructed to defend the roads and were manned by the forces of Breckinridge's command together with reserves, walking wounded from the Lynchburg hospital, and cadets from V. M. I.[93] On the 17th Breckinridge's division was deployed as a curtain around the exposed side of the city, with Vaughn's brigade on the far left. The next day Breckinridge went forward with three of his units, apparently leaving Vaughn in the position of the 17th.[94] The tattered forces from Rockfish Gap were reinforced the next day by Early's troops from Charlottesville, and the Confederates successfully fended off skirmishers sent out by Hunter to test the waters. That night Hunter was intimidated when Early ran locomotives continually in and out of the Lynchburg depot to the sound of bands and cheers, giving the impression that many reinforcements were arriving.[95] As a result, the defenders found the next morning that the Federals had departed the area before dawn.

With his combined forces, Early also left on June 18, to follow and harass Hunter down the Valley and north into Maryland. In his account of these events Early notes that about half his men were barefoot: boots had been ordered, but had not arrived.[96] The dismounted troops, including the Fifty-ninth Tennessee, were unaccustomed to long treks and were especially vulnerable to blistered and bleeding feet on marches that averaged sixteen miles a day. Horses for the dismounted troops under Breckinridge were sent for, but would not arrive for some time.[97] Reuben Clark reports that Breckinridge followed Hunter to Salem, where on June 21 there was an engagement in which the Confederates captured eleven pieces of artillery and some supplies. Skirmishes between units under Early and Hunter are recorded for June 23 at Cove Gap and Sweet Sulphur Springs, West Virginia, and New Castle, Virginia.

Early's forces converged at Staunton on June 27, and here he reorganized them, combining the divisions then under Wharton and Elzey. Because Elzey was ill, an undoubtedly reluctant Early gave command of the new division to Vaughn as senior brigadier. Breckinridge was given a corps that included Vaughn's new command.[98] Carrying out a plan by General Lee to threaten the Federal capitol, Early began preparing for a move on Washington by ordering his commanders to destroy roads, burn bridges and railroad bridges in the Potomac basin of West Virginia and Maryland, and, to the extent possible, to clear out Union forces. At this point Early and his field commanders took separate paths.[99] From June 29 to July 2 Breckinridge marched his troops seventy-six miles.[100] By July 2 Vaughn was nine miles below Winchester, Virginia, and with others of Breckinridge's corps, moved the next day to take Martinsburg, where, it was reported, they "captured several hundred men and great quantities of commissary stores" (fig. 19).[101] Burning railroad bridges as they went, Breckinridge's troops headed for Harpers Ferry, but turned north on discovering well-entrenched Federal forces at the Ferry. The Rebels camped near Sharpsburg on July 5 when Vaughn was again reduced to brigade command, this time in favor of Brigadier General John Echols.[102]

Between July 8 and 9, 1864, all of Early's units came together again and headed toward Washington.[103] At Monocacy Junction, Maryland, on July 9, they met a Federal force under Major General Lew Wallace. In the bloody battle that followed, the larger Confederate army overwhelmed the Federals, who withdrew in disorder.[104] Yet Early's forces, after weeks of marching and fighting, were too tired to continue on into Washington while they had the advantage.[105] For reasons that are not recorded, Vaughn's brigade was commanded at Monocacy by Brigadier General Thomas Smith in General Echols's division.[106] This division, however, did not participate in the fighting,[107] which explains why Reuben Clark's account of Monocacy, although that of an eyewitness, is without reference to combat by his unit. While most of Early's forces crossed the river that night, the men of the Fifty-ninth "camped on the battlefield, with the dead and wounded around us."[108] As at Piedmont, so at Monocacy the Fifty-ninth Tennessee is not mentioned (except by Clark and John Shields) in accounts or on troop lists.

Reuben gives only a cursory review of the next event in which the regiment participated, General Early's famous raid on Washington, July 11–12, 1864, perhaps because Echols's division brought up the rear of the invading forces.[109] General Grant ordered an artillery attack on the Southerners, who responded enough to produce Union casualties, but no full-scale battle resulted. Still, it was an important enough engagement for President Lincoln to have appeared as an observer.[110] After the Confederates withdrew, Clark says, "[w]e then fell back into Virginia. . . ." Shields notes that his unit crossed the Potomac at Leesburg, Virginia, and camped for the night not far from there.[111]

During the next few days, Vaughn's brigade, with Vaughn again in command and again under Breckinridge, kept an eye on Union cavalry in the area between Martinsburg, West Virginia, and Winchester, Virginia.[112] John Shields states that the men of the Fifty-ninth finally received their horses at Winchester.[113] On July 20 Vaughn's brigade served as the rear guard for Major General Stephen D. Ramseur's division in an engagement with Union cavalry under Brigadier General W. W. Averell at Rutherford's Farm, Virginia.[114] Ramseur's information about enemy numbers was faulty, and the Confederates suffered many casualties before the Federals were finally halted. Early blamed Vaughn, who had been watching Averell, for the error in assessing the strength of Union forces.[115]

Clark records that the Fifty-ninth was in the cavalry skirmish with forces led by General George Crook at New Town, Virginia, on July 22.[116] On July 24 Breckinridge attacked the First and Second U.S. Infantry divisions under Crook in the second battle of Kernstown, turned the Federals' flank, and routed them.[117] The Rebels pursued Crook, as Clark states, "down the valley [northward] beyond the Potomac River, capturing supply trains and provisions on the way." An editorial note to the memoir explains that Crook claimed, falsely it seems, that he had retrieved or burned all wagons. In an August 1, 1864, troop list, Vaughn's brigade is shown under the command of Colonel William M. Bradford in yet another division.[118] No reason is given for the changes, but they were temporary, and the brigade was soon back in Breckinridge's corps.

Over a period of several weeks Early pressed the Federals in the lower Valley, effectively carrying out General Lee's plan to expel Union forces from the region.[119] There were skirmishes at Martinsburg and at Hagerstown, Maryland, on July 25 and 29.[120] Men of Vaughn's brigade went into Hagerstown on August 5,[121] and in this town of predominantly Confederate sympathies, Reuben and others found respite from the war in social events at the homes of local people (fig. 20). Elsewhere on the very next day, plans that would result in the ultimate failure of the Confederate's defense of the Valley were set in motion: overall command of Union operations in the Shenandoah was entrusted to the talented and aggressive Major General Philip H. Sheridan.

On August 9, Sheridan marched his troops up the Valley (fig. 16) to Berryville, Virginia, forcing Early to move to Winchester and by August 12 to Fisher's Hill in order to protect his supply lines and avoid being caught between the enemy and the Potomac.[122] The Fifty-ninth Tennessee, with the rest of Vaughn's brigade and Brigadier General John D. Imboden's cavalry, met Brigadier General Alfred T. A. Torbert's Union cavalry in what Early called "a severe fight" at the intersection of the Front Royal and the White Post-New Town roads on August 11, 1864. Torbert used both artillery and dismounted troops to dislodge the Confederates from behind stone walls.[123] From now on, Early would be increasingly on the defensive, and his successes at Lynchburg, in the lower Valley, at Monocacy, and in Washington would be replaced by ever more bitter defeats.

The Confederates encamped at Fisher's Hill until August 17, when both armies began a series of strategic moves in an effort to gain tactical advantage or to deceive the enemy.[124] A number of skirmishes followed as the armies jockeyed for position. By August 21 Vaughn had joined with the cavalry of Major General Lunsford L. Lomax and was advancing northward down the Valley toward Charlestown, West Virginia.[125] On August 22 Vaughn's entire brigade was reported to have only 562 men, comprising fragments of two other brigades, three Tennessee cavalry battalions and one of troops from Georgia. Most of the brigade was then ordered to southwest Virginia, leaving only dismounted troops with Vaughn, including the Fifty-ninth Tennessee.[126] The fighting, much of it in skirmishes, had become an almost daily routine for those who remained in the Valley. In a skirmish of September 2 on the Martinsburg road at Bunker Hill, Vaughn was driven back by Brigadier General Averell's cavalry, which was in turn routed by Major General Robert E. Rodes's Confederate infantry division. Vaughn was wounded in the ankle in this action and was sent home to recuperate. Following his recovery he was given command of troops in East Tennessee, and he initiated what would be his most successful operations.[127] What remained of Vaughn's brigade in the Shenandoah was led by Colonel James W. Gillespie and Lieutenant Colonel Onslow Bean,[128] in Breckinridge's corps.

About September 5, Early settled at Winchester, Virginia, and both he and Sheridan remained quiet until September 18.[129] Sheridan had been moving steadily into a position that would permit an all-out attack on Early's army, and his scouts had been carefully observing Early's moves and positions. The attack took place on September 19 in the battle known as Third Winchester (or Opequon Creek). Again, the Fifty-ninth Tennessee is not mentioned in the official records, but its presence in this battle is confirmed by Reuben Clark and John Shields.[130] Assuming the regiment was with Breckinridge, the Tennesseans, now mounted, began the day at Stephenson's Depot at 6 A.M., when Confederate pickets encountered Federal cavalry that had crossed the Opequon Creek just before dawn. Breckinridge's troops were soon engaged in a fierce fight with the enemy (fig. 17). Early, under attack near Winchester by Sheridan's main force, ordered Breckinridge in as reinforcement for General Ramseur.[131] By 4:30 P.M. Breckinridge was just north of Winchester facing a large massing of Union cavalry on the left flank and the U.S. Eighth Corps in front; by 5 P.M. he was still closer to Winchester.[132] The Confederates were outnumbered more than three to one, and their defeat was as inevitable as it was stunning. With the close of day the battle ended, and Breckinridge was seen riding about recklessly in a mass confusion of men, horses, and artillery, trying to summon a last burst of effort from his exhausted and frightened troops.[133]

The Confederate units fell back during the night of September 19–20 to the previously fortified heights of Fisher's Hill (fig. 18). Here Early deployed an even more reduced force across too wide a line and, as it turned out, at the wrong places along that line.[134] To make matters worse, Breckinridge had left to take command in the Department of Western Virginia and East Tennessee.[135] The men of Vaughn's brigade, under Colonel Bean, were on the left, with Lomax's cavalry. Although Early lacked confidence in his cavalry, he nevertheless put it in critical positions at both Winchester and Fisher's Hill, and in the latter battle, as at Piedmont, these units received the full force of a surprise flanking maneuver by General Crook.[136] By Clark's account, the Fifty-ninth Tennessee was with dismounted cavalry at Fisher's Hill. The sudden descent of Crook's infantrymen down Little North Mountain behind the Confederate's left at about 4 P.M. sent the Rebels into a chaotic retreat, described by one eyewitness as a stampede.[137]

Early's forces retreated to Harrisonburg, Virginia, and thence to the Blue Ridge foothills to reorganize. As Reuben Clark notes, what remained of Vaughn's brigade in the Valley was then ordered to East Tennessee, and on October 13, 1864, fifty of Vaughn's men under Colonel Bean passed through Breckinridge's headquarters at Wytheville, Virginia, on their way to join Vaughn in an encampment near Bristol, Tennessee, on the border with Virginia.[138] When Clark looked back later to the Shenandoah campaign, he saw it as "a very fatiguing and trying one, and scarcely a day passed that there was not some fighting."

In the Bristol area during the month of October, Vaughn had had much success in recruiting men and in regaining absentees, and by the end of the month his brigade had become the largest in Breckinridge's command, with 156 officers and 1,021 men.[139] On October 28, 1864, the Fifty-ninth Tennessee and other units of Vaughn's brigade were attacked at Morristown, Tennessee, by the forces of Brigadier General Alvin C. Gillem, a Tennessean in Union service. Vaughn once again commanded the brigade, and Reuben considered that the general made a serious tactical error in electing to leave a high position to meet Gillem in a field, where the superior Union numbers could accomplish a flanking maneuver. Vaughn was defeated and withdrew in what he himself called a stampede,[140] in the course of which the Tennessee Federals captured many of his men, among them Reuben

Clark. The new commander of Company I was First Lieutenant John B. Shields, whose "Reminiscences" are frequently cited here.[141]

Vaughn's brigade returned for a time to the Bristol area, but on hearing that the Federal Eighth Tennessee regiment was at Greeneville, proceeded there to engage it. On November 11, 1864, Vaughn's men, again temporarily dismounted, advanced on the Federals at Lick Creek before daylight, forcing them to Bull's Gap. At Bull's Gap, General Breckinridge, with reinforcements, took command and the next night, as the Union troops tried to sneak away to Knoxville, he attacked them by moonlight near Russellville and drove them to Morristown, where they retreated in disorder, leaving their wagon train of stores and their artillery behind. The Rebels pursued the Federals as far as Mossy Creek (now Jefferson City), and took more than five hundred prisoners. Vaughn was then left with his men and four artillery pieces "to hold the country," and Breckinridge commended Vaughn and his other commanders for their "zeal and good conduct" in these actions.[142] Vaughn had redeemed himself: the Tennessee merchant had finally mastered the military arts.

Vaughn then returned with his troops to Sullivan County and went into winter camp at Horse Creek.[143] He was now expected to harass Union forces in East Tennessee and southwestern Virginia, preventing them from joining in the effort to take Petersburg and ultimately Richmond.[144] A member of the Fifty-ninth Tennessee later reported engagements at Greeneville, Tennessee, and Marion and Wytheville, Virginia.[145] At Marion, site of an iron foundry, Gillem once again attacked Vaughn on December 16, 1864, again routed him, and pursued him to Wytheville. The Union general claimed he captured Confederate artillery, supply trains, and almost half of Vaughn's men.[146] Yet Vaughn reported on December 22 that his trains were safe, but he does not mention troop numbers.[147] His only other important setback in this last campaign was on December 6, 1864, during the successful series of raids by Major General George Stoneman against Confederate iron and salt mines and works in southwestern

Virginia.[148] Otherwise, General Vaughn was effective in keeping the Federals busy, and by his successful strategies and his dogged pursuit of the aims set out for him, Vaughn also challenged those Confederates, such as General Early, who distrusted his ability to command. Through the end of 1864 and until April 12, 1865, when he learned of Lee's surrender at Appomattox, Vaughn moved his forces about as needed to contain the Federals. In addition to the December actions just noted, in the same month he was also at Hillsville, Virginia, Mount Airy, North Carolina, and Bristol, Tennessee.[149] He was in Athens, Tennessee, on January 28, 1865, and with Major General Joseph Wheeler's cavalry, captured more than twenty members of the U.S. Seventh Tennessee Mounted Infantry before being driven off. A small force from Vaughn's command successfully attacked the Union garrison at Athens on February 20; on the 23rd another detachment took the garrison at Sweet Water, Tennessee, along with much needed horses and equipment belonging to the Second Ohio. The brigade had made camp again at Horse Creek in January 1865, and from about April 1 to April 9 at Wytheville, Virginia.[150]

In a series of reports and letters written in Bristol in February, Vaughn noted that his troops were spread widely to find forage, but that he was also concerned that they leave enough grain for citizen families.[151] He stated that his men had not been paid for nineteen months, were poorly clothed and armed, and kept on the front all the time; there was not even enough paper for requisitions.[152] Obviously, such conditions, although now the norm for the Confederate army, would exacerbate Vaughn's problems of command, yet as he notes, his troop strength was increasing daily, and most of his military actions were successful. Nevertheless, citing difficulties with citizens of East Tennessee, Vaughn wrote that he would "not object to being relieved from this department."[153] In February 1865, Breckinridge was made Confederate secretary of war, and his command passed to Brigadier General John Echols. Vaughn wrote to Breckinridge on February 7 expressing deep regret at the latter's departure, calling him "Kentucky's noblest son."[154] He also asked for Breckinridge's help in obtaining supplies for his troops.

Contradicting John Shields's account, a Union report puts Vaughn's forces at Bristol in early April, 1865,[155] but when news of Lee's surrender arrived on April 12, he was at Christiansburg, Virginia, with Echols, who on March 30 was given command of the Department of Southwestern Virginia when Early was relieved by General Lee.[156] On hearing of the surrender Echols almost immediately disbanded his forces and gave the men permission to return home. Many members of the Fifty-ninth Tennessee left the unit at this time.[157] Others went to Abbeville, South Carolina, where they guarded the rail cars holding Confederate specie from Richmond, then guarded the pontoon bridge over the Savannah River near Abbeville. Shields reported seeing President Jefferson Davis and his staff when they crossed the bridge on their way south. When the rest of the Confederate troops had also crossed, Shields and other members of Company I went to Lexington, Georgia, and thence to Athens, Georgia, where they surrendered and were paroled on May 4, 1865. The next day all of Shields's men left for home, except himself and Lieutenant William H. Long, both of whom had relatives in the area.[158] Meanwhile, Vaughn and other brigade commanders had asked for volunteers to continue on until the war was finally terminated, but only a few hundred men responded. Vaughn was reported at Greeneville, Tennessee, on April 19 with two captains and eighty-four men.[159] Thereafter he headed for Charlotte, North Carolina, promising those who would follow him that he would not engage the enemy; yet he could attract only about two hundred troops.[160]

At Charlotte, Vaughn and his little band joined the escort for Jefferson Davis as the Confederate president and his family made their way south, hoping to escape to a safe haven across the Mississippi. On learning of General Joseph E. Johnston's April 26th surrender to Major General W. T. Sherman, Vaughn refused to take Davis any further than Washington, Georgia, a small town in the northeastern part of the state that became the last central encampment of the Confederate army.¹⁶¹ Davis and his escort arrived there about noon on May 3, and the president left next day. The escort, including Vaughn's troops, remained in Washington, some of them undoubtedly adding to the growing chaos and lawlessness in the streets as units were disbanded and soldiers were left to their own devices to find transportation to their homes. Confederate troops had already begun arriving in Washington by mid-April, ragged, hungry, sick, impoverished, and desperate. Their problems and the problems they created almost overwhelmed Washington's small population of genteel planters, who tried to feed and help them.¹⁶² A company of Union cavalry took charge of Washington on May 5, and the flustered young Federal captain, Lot Abraham, had to contact his superior for instructions on how to receive the numerous contingents of surrendering Confederate troops.¹⁶³ On May 10, General Vaughn's men, along with those of the six other small brigades in the presidential escort, surrendered, stacked their arms, requested and received their paroles, and were permitted to leave with their horses.¹⁶⁴

There is no way of knowing how many, if any, members of the Fifty-ninth Tennessee were among those paroled at Washington; the official accounts say nothing of units below brigade level, or their members, nor are Washington paroles recorded in the Compiled Service Records of the Fifty-ninth. A report of May 5, 1865, states that some officers and men from Vaughn's command had surrendered while still at Greeneville, Tennessee, and asked for surrender terms for the rest of the brigade. They stated that Vaughn was buying a farm in Abbeville, South Carolina, and intended to settle there with his family.¹⁶⁵ A small number of the men from the Fifty-ninth were apparently paroled by the Tenth Michigan Cavalry at Newton, North Carolina, in March and April 1865.¹⁶⁶ The troops of Company I, as noted above, were paroled at Athens, Georgia.

Even before the Shenandoah campaign, physical conditions in the Fifty-ninth Tennessee had deteriorated. In a report of April 29, 1864, written at Bristol, Tennessee, Lieutenant Colonel Archer Anderson, assistant adjutant to General Bragg, summarized the sad state of things in cavalry units of the Department of East Tennessee. Vaughn's brigade was not mentioned, for it was away recruiting horses in North Carolina. Anderson found that in other units weapons and clothing were in bad repair, horses in poor condition from lack of proper feed, bookkeeping in disarray, and there was little evidence of proper training in drilling and tactics.[167] Vaughn's brigade is reviewed in a report of May 6, 1864, by Colonel John B. Sale, military secretary to Confederate headquarters, who stated that the conditions were miserable, that Vaughn should be disciplined or unassigned, and the whole brigade dismounted. Like Anderson, he deplored the Jenifer saddles, which damage the horses' backs and are "worse than worthless."[168] The Fifty-ninth Tennessee escaped direct criticism in Sale's report, for it was in Ashe and Watauga counties, North Carolina, probably to seek forage; grain was growing scarce and transportation difficult in the war-torn South, and "it was easier to bring the cavalry to the corn than the corn to the cavalry."[169] Sale's observations on the brigade would undoubtedly describe the Fifty-ninth, absent or present, for he put the blame on Vaughn, who has "no idea of discipline."[170]

The Compiled Service Records of the Fifty-ninth Tennessee, like those of the entire Confederate army, are notoriously incomplete in both facts and chronology, and the informality of the record keeping produced numerous errors and confusions. For example, a soldier not responding present at roll call was often listed as absent without leave, when in fact he may have been on special duty, sick, or a prisoner of war. Sometimes the true situation was finally revealed, oftentimes not. Thus, overall troop count and troop disposition for any given unit are uncertain. Nevertheless, the numbers culled from the records for the Fifty-ninth Tennessee, inaccurate though they may be, give some idea of what happened to the men who participated in the events just described.

Enlistments: 1373. Killed: 8. Died or killed outside of combat: 71.
Wounded: 10. Captured by the enemy: 176. Deserted or AWOL: 319.
Resigned or discharged: 72. Substitutions: 4. Court martialed: 2

In all or most categories there were probably many more than those recorded in the Compiled Records. Obviously, more than eight were killed or died from their wounds, and more than ten were wounded, especially during the Shenandoah campaign. The most common causes of recorded non-combat deaths in the regiment were dysentery and typhoid fever.[171] A small group of the men were killed in a railroad accident at Chunky Creek, Mississippi, on February 19, 1863.

In these records, and probably in reality, desertion was a major cause of attrition in the ranks of the Fifty-ninth, as it was in numerous regiments, north and south. The causes of desertion from the Fifty-ninth were undoubtedly the usual ones: fear, homesickness, the pleas of destitute and helpless families, hunger, the threat of illness, inadequate clothing, and low morale. Moreover, the Confederacy's first Conscription Act, of April 16, 1862, led many soldiers raised in a states' rights atmosphere to react against this centralizing government action.[172] In the Fifty-ninth Tennessee the greatest number of desertions occurred just after the surrender at Vicksburg, when men were given furloughs, and near the end of the war; this pattern of early-war and late-war desertion was common. Somewhat fewer desertions from the regiment occurred during the Kentucky campaign of 1862. Often prisoners of war took the loyalty oath rather than continue to endure the horrendous conditions of most prison camps or to avoid prison altogether. This last type of desertion is reported on quite a few muster slips of men who were captured while on leave at home in East Tennessee in 1864 and 1865. As in many Confederate units, all the Fifty-ninth's companies included several members of one family, and sometimes all members of such family groups deserted, although not always at the same time. As for capture in combat situations, men of the Fifty-ninth were taken principally in the battle of the Big Black, near Vicksburg, on May 17, 1863, and at the battle of Piedmont on June 5, 1864.

There is no record of reunions of the Fifty-ninth Tennessee. In view of the difficulties Reuben Clark encountered in Knoxville after his release from prison and the attacks on and threats to other Confederate soldiers returning to the area at the war's end,[173] it is likely that those who returned to their old homes stayed quiet and, as much as possible, out of sight for a number of years after the war. In 1889 a Confederate Veterans' Association of Upper East Tennessee was formed in Morristown, with its first reunion in October of that year.[174] By this time, however, many veterans would have died, and others, like Reuben, had left East Tennessee for more friendly regions, never to return. About 1872 Reuben's friends, the Van Dyke family, moved to Rome, Georgia, where Reuben also settled. Perhaps with the publication of Reuben Clark's memoirs, other documents relating to the Fifty-ninth Tennessee will be drawn forth from family and local records to add further to the history of this otherwise unsung but worthy and, from all accounts, rather typical Confederate regiment.

Notes

The following abbreviations are used in the notes:

OR refers to *The War of the Rebellion: A Compilation of the Official Records of the Union and Confederate Armies, 1861–1865*.

ORN refers to *Official Records of the Union and Confederate Navies in the War of the Rebellion*.

INTRODUCTION

1. On transportation problems in East Tennessee to mid-century, see Mary U. Rothrock, ed., *The French Broad-Holston Country. A History of Knox County, Tennessee* (Knoxville: East Tennessee Historical Society, 1946), chap. 9.
2. Rothrock, ed., *The French Broad-Holston Country*, 86– 89. Small paper mills and iron foundries, operating between about 1825 and 1861 in East Tennessee, are described in [John B. Shields] "The Reminiscences of Judge John Brabson Shields (25 Aug. 1840–13 May 1930)," *East Tennessee Roots* 7: 1 (1992): 1–17; Shields was a lieutenant in Reuben Clark's military company. Gary G. Clark kindly informed me of this article.
3. Charles F. Bryan, Jr., " 'Tories' amidst Rebels: Confederate Occupation of East Tennessee, 1861–63," *East Tennessee Historical Society Publications* 60 (1988): 3.
4. William J. MacArthur, Jr., "Knoxville's History: An Interpretation," in *Heart of the Valley: A History of Knoxville, Tennessee*, ed. Lucile Deaderick (Knoxville: East Tennessee Historical Society, 1976), 23.
5. Bryan, "'Tories' amidst Rebels," 19–20; MacArthur, "Knoxville's History: An Interpretation," 24–25.

6. Bryan, " 'Tories' amidst Rebels," presents a good summary of the conditions. See also Thomas W. Humes, *The Loyal Mountaineers of Tennessee* (Knoxville: Ogden Bros. & Co., 1888). Publications of the East Tennessee Historical Society offer several excellent overviews of the region and its history: Rothrock, ed., *The French Broad-Holston Country;* Deaderick, ed., *Heart of the Valley;* and Digby Gordon Seymour, *Divided Loyalties* (rev. ed., Knoxville: East Tennessee Historical Society, 1982), an account of the political situation in the Civil War period. See also Russell Lacy, *Vanquished Volunteers: East Tennessee and Sectionalism from Statehood to Secession* (Johnson City: East Tennessee Univ. Press, 1965), chap. 8.
7. The family came to Tennessee at an unknown date from Augusta County, Virginia. According to U.S. Population Censuses of 1830, 1840, and 1850, Joseph had four children by his first wife, Susan Latham, and four by Martha. I am grateful to Gary Clark and John Grove Peck, Jr., for much information on the family.
8. A large landholding was four hundred to five hundred acres; Fred Arthur Baily, *Class and Tennessee's Confederate Generation* (Chapel Hill: Univ. of North Carolina Press, 1987), 30.
9. The typical log house in East Tennessee was built on piers or on a solid stone foundation, with plank floors, plank or wood shingle roof, and a single stone or brick chimney; John Morgan, *The Log House in East Tennessee* (Knoxville: Univ. of Tennessee Press, 1990), 20–34. He shows, 84–86, that in a number of regions, including East Tennessee, living in a log house often carried a stigma, and, 45, that after the war, all classes of people built frame houses. See also, Baily, *Class and Tennessee's Confederate Generation,* 22.
10. In Grainger County, with a population of 10,962 before the war, there were 199 slave owners and 1,065 slaves; Lacy, *Vanquished Volunteers,* Appendix B.
11. For national backgrounds and religious inclinations of East Tennessee people, see Lacy, *Vanquished Volunteers,* 11.
12. Baily, *Class,* 46–47.
13. Gustavus W. Dyer and John Trotwood Moore, *The Tennessee Civil War Veterans Questionnaires* (Easley, S.C.: Southern Historical Press, 1985) 3: 1302.
14. *Rome [Ga.] City Directory* (Atlanta: Howard & Dozier, 1888), 132, provides the information on these first salaries; Josephine Battey Hollingsworth furnished this reference.
15. On Cowan and Dickinson, see for example, Betsey Beeler Creekmore, *Knoxville* (Knoxville: Univ. of Tennessee Press, 1958), 132; Rothrock, ed., *The French Broad-Holston Country,* 411.
16. Rothrock, ed., *The French Broad-Holston Country,* 106.

17. An R. G. Clark, age 25, is listed as a resident of the McClung home in the 1860 U.S. Census. Although RGC was 27 by November 1860, given his friendship with the McClungs, he and this R. G. Clark are almost certainly one and the same. Another R. G. Clark, age 24, is listed under James W. Bridges, hotel keeper, which may represent Reuben's earlier lodging. John Grove Peck, Jr., kindly informed me of these records.
18. The division of Whigs in Tennessee is discussed in Arthur Charles Cole, *The Whig Party in the South* (Gloucester, Mass.: Peter Smith, 1962), 1, 195.
19. Baily, *Class,* chap. 4, 66, notes that in Tennessee the nonslaveowning gentlemen of modest means were received on equal terms by the wealthy planters and the slave-owners. See also Bertram Wyatt-Brown, *Honor and Violence in the Old South* (Oxford: Oxford Univ. Press), 1986, chap. 3.
20. W. Patton, *Unionism and Reconstruction in Tennessee, 1860–1869* (1934; rpt., Gloucester, Mass.: Peter Smith, 1966), chap. 3, puts excessive stress on class enmities as a cause of the divisions in East Tennessee.
21. Washington D.C., National Archives, Case Files of Applications from Former Confederates for Presidential Pardons, 1865–67, Record Group 94, Tennessee, no. 455.
22. The brief New York period is recorded in a biographical sketch of him in the *Rome City Directory* (Atlanta: Howard & Dozier, 1888), 131.
23. In the petition for pardon he states that he entered military service "about the month of May 1862," which is the date on which he became part of the newly organized Confederate army, as part of the Fifty-ninth Tennessee Infantry regiment.
24. Judith Brockenbrough McGuire, Diary excerpt, in *Heroines of Dixie,* ed. Katharine M. Jones (1955; rpt. New York: Mockingbird, 1974), 34. A number of training camps were established in the Confederacy, and drills of various types helped to keep men fit and to prevent boredom in winter encampments; see for example Larry J. Daniel, *Soldiering in the Army of Tennessee* (Chapel Hill: Univ. of North Carolina Press, 1991), 23–28.
25. Daniel, *Soldiering in the Army of Tennessee,* 13.
26. See Clark's Compiled Service Records, Microfilm (hereafter noted as "M") 268, no. 333.
27. Randolph H. McKim, *A Soldier's Recollections: Leaves from the Diary of a Young Confederate* (Washington, D.C.: Zenger, 1910; 1983).
28. This second charge may have been a verbal one; no documentation for it has been found.
29. Charles Faulkner Bryan, Jr., "The Civil War in East Tennessee: A Social, Political, and Economic Study," Ph.D. dissertation, Univ. of Tennessee, Knox-

ville, 1978, 124, citing *OR* 1.30.2: 550; and *The Knoxville Whig and Rebel Ventilator,* Jan. 9, 1864. Carter was relieved of duty as provost-marshal on Jan. 20, 1865; *OR* 1.65.2: 620.

30. Brownlow's anti-Presbyterian feelings are noted by Thomas B. Alexander, Introduction to William G. Brownlow's *Sketches of the Rise, Progress, and Decline of Secession* (Philadelphia: George W. Childs, 1862; New York: Da Capo, 1968).

31. William Gannaway "Parson" Brownlow (1805–87): a Virginian who moved to Knoxville and became a traveling Methodist preacher, and before the war publisher of the *Knoxville Whig and Independent Journal* (1849–61). As a Unionist, he was forced to flee the city in the early days of the war. After the Union capture of Knoxville, Brownlow returned to edit *The Knoxville Whig and Rebel Ventilator* (1863–65, and longer under his son) and to hound Confederates and their families. See E. Merton Coulter, *William G. Brownlow: The Fighting Parson of the Southern Highlands* (1937; rpt., Knoxville: Univ. of Tennessee Press, 1971).

32. Morgan is not identified. Reynolds is Captain John T. Reynolds, Sixty-fourth North Carolina Regiment, under sentence of death for recruiting in Greene County, Tennessee. A letter of Aug. 7, 1864, from Brigadier General John H. Morgan to General Carter threatens retaliation on Captain Benjamin Rogers of the Tennessee Union Guard if Reynolds is harmed; *OR* 2.7: 561.

33. "Appendix I: The Diary of Jacob Austin Sperry," in Paul W. Prindle, *Ancestry of William Sperry Beinecke* (North Haven, Conn.: Van Dyke Printing Co., 1974) 244–45. I am grateful to Pollyanna Creekmore for making me aware of this interesting document.

34. Brownlow, *Sketches,* opp. 321. The cage scene is reproduced in Seymour, *Divided Loyalties,* 2d ed., 226. Brownlow, *Sketches,* 326–28, 418–19, claims that the daughter asked him to write a letter to General William H. Carroll, Confederate commandant of Knoxville, requesting that Self be spared. On Dec. 27, 1861, Carroll agreed, but kept Self in custody.

35. Benson J. Lossing, *Pictorial History of the Civil War* (Hartford: Thomas Belknap, 1866–77), 2: 38, n. 1. I owe this reference to Steve Cotham of the McClung Historical Collection, Knoxville, Tennessee.

36. An agreement for prisoner exchange was signed by the two belligerents on Sept. 25, 1862. The terms stipulated a "man for man and officer for officer" exchange, except for higher officers, for whom a number of lower rank must be exchanged; K. W. Munden and H. P. Beers, *Guide to Federal Archives Relating to the Civil War* (Washington: National Archives, 1962), 325. The system worked until 1863; see Memoirs, chap. 5, note 1.

37. OR 2.8: 131, 308. The Clark letter mentioned by Ould has not been found, but may be the one RGC told the prison doctor he had written to Breckinridge (chap. 8), and if so, it would have perished when the general's papers burned in a house fire (Munden and Beers, *Guide to Federal Archives Relating to the Civil War*, 136).
38. OR 2.7: 929, 1112.
39. OR 2.8: 389.
40. Alexander Donelson Coffee in a letter to his wife, cited by Clement Eaton, *A History of the Southern Confederacy* (1954; rpt., New York: Collier, 1961), 98.
41. By 1891 there were a variety of accounts of the campaigns in which he participated, including the earlier volumes of *The War of the Rebellion: A Compilation of the Official Records of the Union and Confederate Armies;* studies by Frances Vinton Greene, George E. Pond and A. T. Mahan, in the series collected under the heading *Campaigns of the Civil War*, vols. 4, 6, and 8; Edward A. Pollard, *Southern History of the War* (New York: C. B. Richardson, 1866; New York: Fairfax Press, 1990); and articles in newspapers and periodicals.
42. Mrs. Hollingworth and the editor are granddaughters of Clark's second marriage. The editor's copy will be given to the McClung Historical Collection. The Hollingworth copy measures 8 3/4 by 7 inches and is bound in brown morocco on paperboard; the editor's copy has the same measurements and is similarly bound in dark red. The upper covers of both have a slim border, small cornerpieces, and the title between two stars set vertically, all imprinted in gold; small cruciform decorations in gold ornament the spine. The gilt-edged endpapers are marbled in gold, white, brown, and green-blue.

THE CIVIL WAR EXPERIENCE OF
CAPTAIN REUBEN G. CLARK

Chapter 1

1. Samuel Gill was a prominent merchant and business man of Grainger County, according to Gary Clark of Morristown, Tennessee, who studies families of the region (correspondence of July 4, 1989). In a survey of the 1850 U.S. Census, John Grove Peck, Jr., found a John Clark, age 22, living with Samuel Gill and serving as a clerk in Gill's store. If Gary Clark's genealogies of the Clark family are correct, however, RGC's "eldest brother" would have been Samuel, born between 1820 and 1825 of his father's first marriage.
2. The firm was founded by James Hervey Cowan (1801–71) in 1820. His brother-in-law Perez Dickinson (1813–1901), from a well-known Amherst,

Massachusetts, family, became a partner in 1832 or 1833. See Rothrock, *The French Broad-Holston Country,* 402, 411; also Creekmore, *Knoxville,* 132.
3. This service is never explained, but must have occurred during RGC's sojourn in the Union prison at Knoxville.

Chapter 2

1. John Bell (?1797–1869), a Constitutional Unionist; John Cabell Breckinridge (1821–1875), U.S. representative, senator from Kentucky, and vice-president, then Confederate major general and secretary of war, and for a period in 1864 RGC's commanding officer; Abraham Lincoln (1809–65). Stephen A. Douglas (1813–61) was nominated by those loyalist Democrats who refused to allow a slave code in the party's platform.
2. Major (later Brigadier General) Robert Anderson (1805–71): USA; a native of Kentucky who remained loyal to the Union. As commandant of Fort Sumter in Charleston Harbor, it was he who surrendered the fort on April 13, 1861, after many hours of bombardment by secessionists.
3. Douglas was not an independent, but as noted, represented a branch of the Democratic Party. He is most famous for his debates with Lincoln over state sovereignty in the matter of slavery.
4. Brigadier General Pierre Gustave Toutant Beauregard (1818–93): CSA; the Southern hero of Fort Sumter; also known for his arrogance and sartorial splendor.
5. Jefferson Finis Davis (1808–89) of Kentucky and Mississippi. Before the formation of the Confederacy, Davis has served the U.S. government as secretary of war.
6. John Caldwell Calhoun (1782–1850) of South Carolina; advocate of states' rights, he warned of the possibility of civil war.
7. John C. Vaughn (1824–75); for more on Vaughn, see Appendix.
8. RGC's enlistment in the Third Tennessee is recorded in a penciled note in the Hollingsworth copy of the memoirs. For the regiment's brigade and division, see *OR* 1.1.2: 187, 470.

Chapter 3

1. Washington, D.C., National Archives, Record Group 109, Compiled Service Records, M268, no. 125 (Record of Events dated July 8, 1861).
2. Brigadier (later Major) General Arnold Elzey (né Jones; 1816–71): CSA, formerly USA.

NOTES FOR PAGES 11-13   121

3. Colonel (later Lieutenant General) Ambrose Powell Hill (1825–65). For forces in the brigade, *OR* 1.2: 187.
4. I am grateful to Ross D. Netherton for interpreting these statements. On a map of northeastern Virginia compiled in the Topographic Engineers Office, Division Hdq. of General Irvin McDowell, Arlington, Aug. 1, 1862, he notes two small churches on the Orange and Alexandria railroad line. The first, with a steeple, is St. Mary's Roman Catholic Church, constructed in 1858. The older church would then be the structure built in 1766–68 by a Captain Payne, in which box seats as described by RGC would be expected. George Washington served for a time on the vestry of Payne's church. Netherton says that it is possible that some of the Fairfax family also attended the Payne church before the Revolution, which may have led to RGC's apparent misinformation as to the sponsor of the building.
5. Compiled Service Records, M268, no. 125, Record of Events slip of Company A, Fifty-ninth Tennessee for Sept.–Oct. 1861. B. F. Cooling, *Symbol, Sword, and Shield. Defending Washington during the Civil War* (Hamden, Conn.: Archon, 1975), 73–74, notes that Confederate outposts "dotted Munson's and Miner's Hills," from which positions the spires of Washington could be seen. To their chagrin, Union forces learned after the Rebels withdrew from the hills, near the end of September, that many of the "cannon" were logs painted black.
6. See for example, Clement Eaton, *A History of the Southern Confederacy* (New York: Collier, 1954), 153.
7. Colonel James Burch Cooke; see Appendix.
8. Brigadier (then Major) General Edmund Kirby Smith (1824–93): CSA, later commander of the Department of Trans-Mississippi.
9. [Shields], "Reminiscences," 5.
10. For documentation on all references to the Fifty-ninth Tennessee, see the regimental history in the Appendix.
11. *OR* 1.16.2: 719. Brigadier (later Major) General Carter Littlepage Stevenson (1817–88): CSA.
12. Compiled Service Records, M268, no. 333.
13. Compiled Service Records, M268, no. 333: Record of Events for Sept.–Oct. 1862.
14. General Braxton Bragg (1817–76): CSA; commander of the Army of Tennessee.
15. The Kentucky campaign was not so brief, lasting some two months.
16. Compiled Service Records, M268, no. 333: Record of Events for Sept.–Oct. 1862.

17. Stevenson's orders are dated Dec. 18; *OR* 1.20.2: 453.
18. Dalton was a major encampment site at the junction of several important Southern rail lines. See Robert C. Black III, *The Railroads of the Confederacy* (Chapel Hill: Univ. of North Carolina Press, 1952), map opp. 7.
19. Major Charles M. Alexander died Oct. 23, 1862 (Compiled Service Records, M268, no. 333.)
20. Officers on both sides below the rank of general were elected by vote of their units until at least 1863, the South longer than the North; the system did not always place the best men in leadership positions; James M. McPherson, *Battle Cry of Freedom: The Civil War Era* (New York: Ballantine, 1988), 327–28.
21. Lucy Cowan, daughter of James H. Cowan of Knoxville. As a widow she and her sister Mary kept house for their widower uncle, Perez Dickinson, RGC's former employer; see Creekmore, *Knoxville,* 135.
22. John D. Milligan, *Gunboats Down the Mississippi* (Annapolis: U.S. Naval Institute, 1965), 79.
23. Brigadier General John Alexander McClernand (1812–90): USA. RGC is incorrect here: Major General William T. Sherman commanded Union forces in this battle; McClernand did not replace him until Jan. 4, 1863; *OR* 1.17.1: 689.
24. Major General Martin Luther Smith (1819–66): CSA; at this time commandant of the Confederate defenders of Vicksburg.
25. The battle is described by George W. Morgan, "The Assault on Chickasaw Bluffs," in *Battles and Leaders of the Civil War,* ed. R. U. Johnson and C. D. Buel (New York, 1884–1888; rpt., New York: Yoseloff, 1963) 3: 462–70; and D. Alexander Brown, "Battle of Chickasaw Bluffs," *Civil War Times Illustrated* 9: 4 (1970): 4–9, 44–48.
26. Commander (later Rear Admiral) David Dixon Porter (1813–91): USN; commander of the Mississippi Squadron. See Milligan, *Gunboats Down the Mississippi,* 94–96 and passim.
27. Samuel Carter III, *The Final Fortress: the Campaign for Vicksburg 1862–1863* (New York: St. Martin's Press, 1980), 99, citing Porter, *Naval History of the Civil War* (New York: Sherman, 1886), 294. In his report of this battle, Sherman took note of the torrential rains of that night; *OR* 1.17.1: 608. Commander David Dixon Porter, a key Union figure in the river battle for Vicksburg, wrote that the "level lands were inundated, and there were three feet of water in the swamps. . . ." The map in Brown, "Battle at Chickasaw Bluffs," 8, shows a densely wooded area north of Vicksburg in the direction of the bluffs.
28. Carter L. Stevenson.
29. National Archives, Record Title G.O.29, Dept. of Mississippi and

East Louisiana, Jan. 29, 1863. On Feb. 28, 1863, Cooke resigned his commission on medical grounds and left the service; Compiled Service Records, M268, no. 333.

30. Colonel William L. Eakin, of Madisonville, Tennessee, who was to command the Fifty-ninth Tennessee until his capture in June 1864.
31. Colonel (later Brigadier General) Alexander W. Reynolds (1816–76): CSA.
32. OR 1.16.2: 985; 1.24.3: 612.
33. Edwin C. Bearss, *The Vicksburg Campaign*, 3 vols. (Dayton, Ohio: Morningside House, 1985–86), 1: 351. It is likely that at the river end of the rifle-pit line and in trenches near the river, the erosion that would eventually submerge the whole area of the fort had already begun, revealing the poorly buried Confederate dead. The *Arkansas Gazette* for Dec. 2, 1900, noted that the U.S. dead were removed to national cemeteries, but Confederate graves were being obliterated; see Edwin C. Bearss and Lenard E. Brown, *The Post of Arkansas, 1804–1863* (Washington: Office of History and Historic Architecture, Eastern Service Center, 1971), 284. For this information I am grateful to the Arkansas Post National Memorial ranger, Eddie Wells.
34. Captain (later Admiral) David Glasgow Farragut (1801–70): USN; a Tennessee native, but supporter of the Union, who at the time commanded the West Gulf Blockading Squadron.
35. Commander S. P. Lee: USN.
36. These events are fully described in Bearss, *The Vicksburg Campaign*.
37. Lawrence Lee Hewitt, *Port Hudson, Confederate Bastion on the Mississippi* (Baton Rouge: Louisiana State Univ. Press, 1987), describes and documents the strategic role of Port Hudson for both sides. Also, David C. Edmonds, *The Guns of Port Hudson*, 2 vols. (Lafayette, La.: Acadiana Press, 1983).
38. Compiled Service Records M268, no. 333, pay slip dated Jan. 31, 1863. For Smith, M268, no. 336.
39. USS "Queen of the West," a freighter fitted out for ramming. She was commanded by a nineteen-year-old dare-devil, Colonel Charles Rivers Ellet. See most recently, Bearss, *The Vicksburg Campaign*, 1: 618–21; also Milligan, *Gunboats*, 123–24, and ORN 1.24.217–19.
40. He could have read accounts of the action in Pollard, *Southern History of the War*, 571–73, or A. J. Mahan, *The Gulf and Inland Waters* (New York: Charles Scribner's Sons, 1888), 127–28. The episode is described in Bearss, *The Vicksburg Campaign*, 1: 641–43, and Milligan, *Gunboats*, 124–26.
41. USS "Hartford," a screw sloop, and Farragut's flagship; Patricia L. Faust, ed., *Historical Times Illustrated Encyclopedia of the Civil War* (New York: Harper & Row, 1986), 347, records only 24 guns. The Confederates were building a

large artillery enclosure (casement) on the heights at Warrenton, and Farragut had shelled it on March 21 and 23; *ORN* 1.20: 8, 16, 764.

42. Hewitt, *Port Hudson,* 74.
43. Farragut had requested that the two rams join him, and he shelled the Warrenton batteries to aid the rams' downstream passage; *ORN* 1.20: 19, 25, 764. The admiral's aim was to cut off Confederate supply shipping in the Red River; *ORN* 1.20: 14.
44. Brigadier (later Major) General Ulysses Simpson Grant (1822–85): USA; at this time commander of the Army of the Tennessee.
45. Edwin C. Bearss, *Decision in Mississippi* (Jackson: Miss. Commission on the War Between the States, 1962), 148–52.
46. *OR* 1.24.1: 36.
47. Brigadier General Edward D. Tracy (1833–62): CSA; RGC confuses Tracy at Port Gibson with Lloyd Tilghman at Champion Hill.
48. Brigadier General John Clifford Pemberton (1814–81): CSA; commander of the Department of Mississippi and East Louisiana. A Northerner by birth, Pemberton augmented Southern suspicions of him by his domineering personality and unpolished manner; Stanley F. Horn, *The Army of Tennessee* (Norman: Univ. of Oklahoma Press, 1953), 211–12. Bearss, *The Vicksburg Campaign,* 3: 1314, appears to agree with President Davis that when Pemberton decided, against orders, not to abandon the city, he had only gambled and lost.
49. See Edwin C. Bearss, "Battle at Champion Hill: Sealing the Fate of Vicksburg," *Strategy and Tactics* 103 (1985): 21–24, and his recent *The Vicksburg Campaign,* 2: chaps. 30–35.
50. Neither Edwin C. Bearss nor Terrence J. Winschel, historian at the Vicksburg National Military Park, has seen any other reference to a general appeal; I am grateful to both for their comments. Pemberton's May 12th letter to his troops is printed in Bearss, *The Vicksburg Campaign* 2: 482.
51. The retreat is described in General Stevenson's report, *OR* 1.24.2: 97–98.
52. Bearss, *Decision,* 226.
53. Some sense of the losses during the period of the campaign's great battles is gained from troop lists: on March 31, 1863, Reynolds's brigade had 183 officers and 2,422 men, and on June 25 it had 163 officers and 1,950 men; *OR* 1.24.3: 702, 979.
54. Major General William Wing Loring (1818–86): a division commander under Pemberton during the Vicksburg campaign. He was field commander of the entire Confederate force during this battle; Bearss, *Decision,* 222.

55. Loring's escape is described by Bearss, *Decision*, 288–90 and *The Vicksburg Campaign*, 2: 635–37. With his unit, Loring left Pemberton's command altogether and joined the forces of General Joseph E. Johnston at Jackson, Miss. For the actions of Tilghman's brigade, S. H. Lockett, "The Defense of Vicksburg," in *Battles and Leaders*, ed. Johnson and Buel, 487.
56. OR 1.24.1: 266 and 1.24.2: 98, 101–109, 143; Calvin Smith's diary in Carnes, "We Can Hold Our Ground," *Civil War Times Illustrated* (April 1985): 28–29; also Bearss, *Decision*, 243–46, 285–86, and *The Vicksburg Campaign*, 2: 587, 629–30. More details are given in the Appendix.

Chapter 4

1. OR 1.24.2: 355, Reynolds's report; Bearss, *The Vicksburg Campaign*, 3: 760, map.
2. An account of this attack is in Bearss, *The Vicksburg Campaign*, 3: 761–73. Another Union charge took place on May 22; Bearss, 3: chaps. 40–41.
3. Lockett, "The Defense of Vicksburg," 489. During the battle of Port Hudson, another Union general, Nathaniel P. Banks, had left dead and wounded on the battlefield for days. In this instance, Confederates asked for a truce, collected the decomposing bodies, and took them to the Federals; John D. Winters, *The Civil War in Louisiana* (Baton Rouge: Louisiana State Univ. Press, 1963), 274.
4. OR 1.24.3: 348–49. Other commanders gave similar assessments, in response to an inquiry from Pemberton; Bearss, *Decision*, 435–36.
5. OR 1.24.3: 982–83. Bearss, *Decision*, 435, cautions that this letter might have been Union "disinformation."
6. Calvin Smith's account of the hardships is much like Reuben's; Carnes, "'We Can Hold Our Ground'," 28–31. The constant bombardment is described by a woman in Vicksburg in Henry Steele Commager, *The Blue and the Gray* (Indianapolis: Bobbs-Merrill, 1950), vol. 1: 662–68.
7. Captain F. O. Claiborne, Third Maryland Battery in Reynolds's Fourth Brigade.
8. Daniel, *Soldiering in the Army of Tennessee*, chap. 5, discusses the issue of sickness in the Confederate army.
9. Lockett, "The Defense of Vicksburg," 489. The captured units are listed in OR 1.23.2: 324–25.
10. Narratives by Union soldiers suggest that the sharing of food was spontaneous and sporadic, not strategic; Bearss, *Decision*, 447, and *The Vicksburg Campaign*, 3: 1300. In any case, Grant permitted it.

Chapter 5

1. Parole: French for "word," a captured soldier's word that, if released, he would refrain from further combat until officially exchanged for a prisoner from the other side. Before long, however, huge numbers of prisoners on both sides made the system overly complex; and the U.S. government saw that an end to parole and exchange would exacerbate the South's chronic shortage of troops. The Confederacy—and RGC in chapter 8—used the North's abandonment of the system as an explanation for the overcrowding, starvation, and death by exposure at the notorious prison at Andersonville, Georgia, saying it lacked the funds to properly house and care for so many prisoners. For a summary, see Faust, ed., *Historical Times Encyclopedia,* 558.
2. Bearss, *Decision,* 451–52, and *OR* 1.24.3: 1014.
3. Major General Simon Bolivar Buckner (1821–1914): CSA; then in command of the Department of East Tennessee.
4. Major General Ambrose Everett Burnside (1824–81): USA; then commander of the Department of the Ohio.
5. *OR* 2.6.280.
6. General Joseph Eggleston Johnston (1807–91): CSA, at this time commander of the Department of the West.
7. The Battle of Chickamauga, won by the Confederates, took place near Dalton. RGC is incorrect in placing Johnston at Dalton in September: he did not arrive there until Dec. 26, 1863; see Jeffrey N. Lash, *Destroyer of the Iron Horse. General Joseph E. Johnston and Confederate Rail Transport 1861–1865* (Kent, Ohio: Kent State Univ. Press, 1991), 104, 107. Yet a part of Johnston's Department of the West army had reinforced Bragg and were indeed at Dalton; McPherson, *Battle Cry of Freedom,* 671.
8. Thomas A. Cleage married Penelope S. Van Dyke on Sept. 15, 1856; Reba Bayless Boyer, ed., "Marriage Records of McMinn County, Tennessee 1820–1870," typescript, McClung Historical Collection, p. 56. Judge Thomas Nixon Van Dyke (b. 1803), of "Prospect Hill," Athens, Tennessee, and Rome, Georgia; see his "The Van Dyke Genealogy," typescript, 1872, on deposit at the Library of Congress and the Rome-Floyd County Library, Rome, Georgia.
9. Frances Lavinia Van Dyke, daughter of Judge Thomas Nixon Van Dyke, whose "The Van Dyke Genealogy" is cited above.
10. Probably Mary Smith, daughter of Judge Van Dyke's sister Mary H. (Mrs. William R. Smith) of Mineral Point, Wisconsin. Judge Van Dyke's children and wife were exiled from Knoxville by Federal authorities during the war and lived for a time with the Smiths; the judge was imprisoned in Ohio; see Judge Van Dyke, "The Van Dyke Genealogy," 7.

11. John B. Lindsley, *The Military Annals of Tennessee. Confederate* (Nashville: J. J. Lindsley & Co., 1886), 140, and *OR* 1.31.2: 662.
12. Major General George Henry Thomas (1816–70): USA; commanded the Army of the Cumberland under General William T. Sherman.
13. In Black, *The Railroads of the Confederacy*, only Federal destruction of trains and roadbeds is described, but the Confederates also engaged in such activities.
14. *OR* 1.31.1: 255.
15. Lieutenant General James Longstreet (1825–1904): CSA; commanded the I Corps, Army of Northern Virginia.
16. A Northern account of the retreat, *OR* 1.131.1: 384, does not suggest panic.
17. Lieutenant General Thomas Jonathan Jackson (1824–63): CSA; commander of the II Corps, Army of North Virginia, and a brilliant tactician.
18. Captain John A. Gray, of the First Tennessee Cavalry, USA; Regimental Muster Roll.
19. The frequent harassment and pillaging by radicals, opportunists, and just plain criminals on both sides is described in Bryan, "The Civil War in East Tennessee," 132–39.
20. A small group of undisciplined soldiers in the command of Brigadier General Felix H. Robertson massacred the prisoners and wounded among black Union troops during a lull in the battle (Oct. 2, 1864); see Faust, ed., *Historical Times Encyclopedia*, 654. An historian of Vaughn's Third Tennessee Infantry stated correctly, "Atrocities were attributed to this brigade which should have been charged to outlaws," referring to these incidents; Lindsley, *The Military Annals of Tennessee. Confederate*, 141.

Chapter 6

1. Major General David Hunter (1802–66): USA; commander of the Department of West Virginia.
2. The events surrounding the battle of Piedmont are described by Marshall Moore Brice, *Conquest of a Valley* (Charlottesville: Univ. Press of Virginia, 1965), chaps. 5–7.
3. Brice, *Conquest of a Valley*, 57 and 60, is unaware that the Fifty-ninth Tennessee was part of Vaughn's unit in this battle.
4. *OR* 1.37.1: 95.
5. Brigadier General William Edmondson "Grumble" Jones (1824–64): CSA; a tough cavalry officer who commanded the Department of West Virginia. Brice, *Conquest of a Valley*, 79, notes a confusion in communication between Jones and cavalry forces on his right.

6. The gap is described by Brice, 61, 73, 79; see also Joseph W. A. Whitehorn, "Piedmont," in *The Civil War Battlefield Guide*, ed. Frances H. Kennedy (Boston: Houghton Mifflin, 1990), 233.
7. Brice, *Conquest of a Valley*, 72–73.
8. Possibly Jacob M. Hays of Company C, who is recorded only in 1863 and as a captain; Compiled Service Records, M268, no. 334.
9. General Hunter's report also notes that some of the Confederate troops were, as he put it, driven over the bank and into the river; OR 1.37.1: 95. Lieutenant Wilson is unidentified.
10. Brice, *Conquest of a Valley*, 72.
11. Brice, *Conquest of a Valley*, 79. Robert K. Krick, "'The Cause of All My Disasters': Jubal A. Early and the Undisciplined Valley Cavalry," in *Struggle for the Shenandoah*, ed. Gary W. Gallagher (Kent, Ohio: Kent State Univ. Press, 1991), attributes the lack of response to mere ineptitude. Although neither Imboden nor Vaughn was known for his military prowess, both were experienced leaders and not given to avoiding battle; Brice's explanation appears the more credible.
12. Major General John Cabell Breckinridge (1821–75): CSA; a Kentucky Unionist, he was vice-president of the United States under James Buchanan, and the Democrats' presidential candidate in 1860. In consequence of the secession movement in the South, he was suspected of treason against the United States and forced to flee Washington. He was one of the Confederacy's most talented generals, and one of the handsomest. See William C. Davis's fine biography, *Breckinridge, Statesman, Soldier, Symbol* (Baton Rouge: Louisiana State Univ. Press, 1974). For Breckinridge and the Fifty-ninth Tennessee, see Appendix.
13. OR 1.37.1: 95.
14. OR 37,1: 151; Brice, *Conquest of a Valley*, 82, 88–89, 95, 99.
15. Davis, *Breckinridge*, 439.
16. Davis, *Breckinridge*, 439; Brice, *Conquest of a Valley*, 117.
17. The battle of Lynchburg is described by Brice, *Conquest of a Valley*, chap. 11; also by Frank E. Vandiver, *Jubal's Raid: General Early's Famous Attack on Washington in 1864* (New York, Toronto, London: McGraw-Hill, 1960), 53–58.
18. Lieutenant General Jubal Anderson Early (1816–94): CSA; a member of the Virginia gentry, but known for his acerbic tongue and unsavory manner. His memoirs, *Narrative of the War Between the States* (Philadelphia: Lippincott, 1912; rpt. with introd. by Gary Gallagher, New York: Da Capo Press, 1989), is a major source of information on the Shenandoah campaign. See also Appendix.

19. Brice, *Conquest of a Valley*, 120.
20. B. Long, *The Civil War Day by Day* (Garden City, N.Y.: Doubleday, 1971), 528.
21. Major General Lewis Wallace (1827–1905): USA; commander of the Middle Department; he later wrote the novel *Ben Hur* (1880).
22. On the battle of Monocacy, see Benjamin Franklin Cooling, *Jubal Early's Raid on Washington, 1864* (Baltimore: Nautical and Aviation Publishing Co., 1989), 61–81.
23. Hunter followed the orders of General Ulysses S. Grant, that "the valley, from Winchester up to Staunton . . . will have little in it for man or beast"; OR 1.63.1: 30–31. These activities are vividly described by General John Imboden in "Fire, Sword, and the Halter," in *Annals of the War . . . in the Philadelphia Weekly Times* (Philadelphia: Times Publishing Co., 1897), 177–81, rpt. in *The Blue and the Gray*, ed. Henry Steele Commager (Indianapolis: Bobbs-Merrill, 1950), vol. 2: 1040–42.
24. See General Jubal Anderson Early, *A Memoir of the Last Years of the War* (Toronto: C. W. Button, 1867), 67–68, 70 n., 402, and OR 1.43.1: 753. On the burning of Chambersburg see, most recently, Theodore Alexander et al., eds., *Southern Revenge: Civil War History of Chambersburg, Pennsylvania* (Sheppensburg, Pa.: White Mane and Chambersburg Chamber of Commerce, 1989).
25. F. Cooling, *Jubal Early's Raid*, 145.
26. This purpose is confirmed in OR 1.37.1: 346.
27. Cooling, *Jubal Early's Raid*, 102–110, 146–151.
28. New Town, now Stephens City, is located about 12 miles southwest of Winchester.
29. OR 1.37.1: 171.
30. Samuel L. West, who enlisted in Company I as a sergeant at Morristown, May, 1862; Compiled Service Records, M268, no. 336.
31. For Union reports of this battle, OR 1.37.1: 286, 292–94 (General Crook).
32. Crook, OR 1.37.1: 286, states that he retrieved all artillery and wagons, and those wagons that had been cut loose were burned. Moreover, although Early had just defeated him, Crook brushed off any further threat by his Rebel opponent, noting that Early's troops "are in no condition to make any hard marches." Another Union report, OR 1.37.1: 292–94, corroborates Clark's claim that supplies were captured.
33. Major General Philip H. Sheridan (1831–88): USA, at that time a major general of volunteers and commander of the Army of the Shenandoah.
34. For an account of Early's troop movements, see Jeffry D. Wert, *From Win-*

chester to Cedar Creek: The Shenandoah Campaign of 1864 (New York: Simon & Schuster–Touchstone, 1987), chap. 2.

35. On Sept. 17, Early had taken half his infantry to Martinsburg, not to encounter Sheridan but to thwart rumored repair of the railroad there (there was none). In doing so, he split his army, fatigued the troops by a forced return march, and barely made it back to Winchester to reorganize his forces to meet a major Union attack; Wert, *From Winchester to Cedar Creek*, 44–45. For this battle, see also Joseph P. Cullen, "The Battle of Winchester," in *Battle Chronicles of the Civil War*, ed. James M. McPherson (New York: Collier-Macmillan, 1989), vol. 4: 84–96.

36. Johnston, then a brigadier and commander at Harpers Ferry, withdrew June 15, 1861, before a superior Union force; Pollard, *Southern History of the War*, 87–88..

37. Major General George B. McClellan (1826–85): USA, commander of the Army of the Potomac.

38. Wert, *From Winchester to Cedar Creek*, does not list Vaughn's brigade at Winchester or the subsequent battle at Fisher's Hill.

39. Breckinridge's morning actions are described in Early, *Narrative*, 424; Wert, *From Winchester to Cedar Creek*, 75–78; Edward J. Stackpole, *Sheridan in the Shenandoah* (New York: Bonanza, 1961), 193, 198; and noted in the *Atlas to Accompany the Official Records of the Union and Confederate Armies*, comp. C. D. Cowles (Washington: Government Printing Office, 1891–95; London and New York: Thomas Yoseloff, 1958), 99 no. 1.

40. On the flanking maneuver, Wert, *From Winchester to Cedar Creek*, 84. The dust and confusion are described in a famous passage in John B. Gordon, *Reminiscences of the Civil War* (New York: Charles Scribner's Sons, 1904), 322.

41. I. G. Bradwell, "The Battle of Fisher's Hill," *Confederate Veteran* 28 (1920): 338; Jeffry D. Wert, "Fisher's Hill," in *Battle Chronicles of the Civil War*, ed. McPherson, 4: 97–107.

42. Early, *A Memoir*, 118, stated his losses as less than 4,000.

43. Major General Robert Emmett Rodes (1829–64): CSA; one of Early's most revered officers; see Early, *A Memoir*, 91.

44. Wert, *From Winchester to Cedar Creek*, 119.

45. Wert, *From Winchester to Cedar Creek*, 110, and Bradwell, "The Battle of Fisher's Hill," 338. Bradwell considered the thin deployment a fatal mistake, noting that his former commander, Stonewall Jackson, had passed up Fisher's Hill in 1862, when his forces were insufficient to defend the location.

46. Lieutenant Colonel Onslow Bean. Vaughn was wounded in an engagement at Bunker Hill, Virginia, on Sept. 2, 1864 (Brice, *Conquest of a Valley*, 131;

OR 1.43.1: 572), and Bean commanded the brigade until it returned to Tennessee (OR 1.39.1: 848). Vaughn was sent home on Sept. 5 and given command of troops in East Tennessee; William Frayne Amann, ed., *Personnel of the Civil War I: The Confederate Armies* (New York and London: Thomas Yoseloff, 1961), 1: 361. See also Appendix.

47. Corporal James Croft McCarty, who enlisted as a private in Company I at Noes Ferry, Tennessee, Oct. 5, 1862 (Compiled Service Records M268, no. 335).
48. *Atlas to Accompany the Official Records*, 99, no. 2.
49. This famous maneuver is described by Wert, *From Winchester to Cedar Creek*, 119–23.
50. George S. Pond, *The Shenandoah Valley in 1864* (New York: Charles Scribner's Sons, 1883), 186 n.1.
51. Early, *Narrative*, 429.
52. Bradwell, "The Battle of Fisher's Hill," 338.
53. Ibid.
54. Unidentified.
55. Wert, *From Winchester to Cedar Creek*, 133.
56. Enoch C. Beeler enlisted as a private at Morristown (Compiled Service Records, M268, no. 333).
57. Wert, *From Winchester to Cedar Creek*, 134.
58. Dyer and Moore, *The Tennessee Civil War Veterans Questionnaires*, 4: 1382.
59. Unidentified.
60. John Van Dyke: son of Judge Thomas Nixon Van Dyke; he enlisted as a first lieutenant in A Company at Knoxville and was promoted to captain March 30, 1863 (Compiled Service Records, M268, no. 336). After his death he was buried in a private cemetery near Darksville (T. N. Van Dyke, "The Van Dyke Genealogy," 6).
61. South Carolina socialite Mary Chesnut's hospitality to Confederate officers was legendary; see Mary Boykin Chesnut, *A Diary from Dixie*, ed. Ben Ames Williams (Boston: Houghton Mifflin, 1949), passim. For other examples, Eliza Frances Andrews, *The War-Time Journal of a Georgia Girl 1864–1865* (Macon: Ardivan Press, 1960), 180–217.
62. Samuel Hickle enlisted at 17 as a private. He is listed as a courier for General Reynolds (presumably Alexander W. Reynolds, later his brigade commander) in Nov. 1862. Hickle was brevetted second lieutenant in Feb. 1865 (Compiled Service Records, M268, no. 334).
63. Robert Deaderick Van Dyke, Mary Hamilton Van Dyke Battey, Margaret Josephine Van Dyke Inman. The Van Dykes were typical of many East Tennessee Rebel families who were forced by local antagonism toward former

Confederates to move away from the area at the end of the war. The date of Judge Van Dyke's move to Rome, Georgia, is unknown, but must have been sometime after 1872, when he wrote "The Van Dyke Genealogy" in Athens, Tennessee.

64. Major Richard Smith Van Dyke, son of Judge Van Dyke; he graduated from the College of New Jersey (Princeton) in 1861, according to Judge Van Dyke, "The Van Dyke Genealogy," 5. He was captain of Company C, First Tennessee Cavalry, and then a regimental major until his death; see John B. Lindsley, ed., *The Military Annals of Tennessee, Confederate*, 606–7; Bearss, *The Vicksburg Campaign*, 3: 965.

65. OR 1.37: 171.

66. If this took place July 25, Vaughn's whole brigade was in the area, as shown in the *Atlas to Accompany the Official Records*, 82: 11, which calls this a "cavalry action."

67. Brigadier General William Terry (1824–88): CSA, commanding a brigade in General John B. Gordon's division of the Second Corps, under General Early.

68. Early, *Narrative*, 402, provides the date. See also OR 1.43.1: 753 for Vaughn's advance to Hagerstown.

69. Most likely the daughter of George Schley, a lawyer and state senator of Hagerstown, Maryland, and his wife Mary Sophia Hall. They had three daughters: the youngest Eliza (Mrs. Joseph F. Stellman of Brookline, Massachusetts), the eldest Mrs. Washington Bowie, and the third unmarried; see J. Thomas Scharf, *History of Western Maryland*, 2 vols. (Philadelphia: Louis H. Everts, 1882), 1128–29, who names only Eliza. My thanks to the Washington County Free Library of Hagerstown for this reference.

70. Robert Mercer Taliaferro Hunter (1809–87): a Whig; Speaker of the U.S. House of Representatives 1839–41, senator 1847–61.

71. Probably Jonathan Hager (1796–1864), who made his fortune by milling flour; see Thomas J. C. Williams, *A History of Washington County Maryland* (Hagerstown, 1906; Baltimore: Regional Publishing Co., 1968), 1162.

72. Clement Eaton, *A History of the Southern Confederacy*, 96.

73. Probably 2d Lieutenant James M. King, Sixteenth Tennessee Cavalry, Company B, in Vaughn's brigade; *Tennesseans in the Civil War*, 2 vols. (Nashville: Civil War Centennial Commission of Tennessee, 1964; rpt. Knoxville: Univ. of Tennessee Press, 1985), vol. 2: 237.

74. Lindsley, *The Military Annals of Tennessee, Confederate*, 143.

75. Fifty of Vaughn's men were seen on Oct. 13 at headquarters at Wytheville, Virginia, headed for Tennessee; OR 1.39.3: 819.

Chapter 7

1. Brigadier General Alvan Cullen Gillem (1830–75): USA; a central Tennessean.
2. Gillem describes the action in *OR* 1.39.1: 845–46.
3. *OR* 1.39.1: 845.
4. Davis, *Breckinridge*, 457, 464–68. These matters are discussed in the Appendix.
5. Probably Colonel James E. Carter, who commanded the First Tennessee Cavalry in Vaughn's brigade; *Tennesseans in the Civil War* 2: 81.
6. Brownlow's *Knoxville Whig and Rebel Ventilator*, Nov. 2, 1864, 2, called it "an interesting fight . . . between a brigade of East Tennessee patriots and a brigade of East Tennessee traitors. . . . It was exclusively a Tennessee fight." Vaughn himself described the Confederate retreat as a stampede; *OR* 1.39.1: 851.
7. An unidentified Tennessee Union officer.
8. Colonel Joseph H. Parsons: USA; commander of the Ninth Tennessee Cavalry; *Tennesseans in the Civil War* 1: 342.
9. Colonel William H. Sneed (1812–69): law partner of Oliver Perry Temple and Judge Connelly F. Trigg, the latter to play a decisive role in RGC's life. See Rothrock, ed., *The French Broad-Holston Country*, 487–88.
10. Gillem stated that he captured 226 Confederates, including 19 officers. He claimed that Vaughn was wounded in the battle, but this assertion is not supported elsewhere. See *OR* 1.39.1: 845–46.
11. Lieutenant D. M. Nelson: USA; a member of General Gillem's staff (*OR* 1.39.1: 846), and a son of Thomas A. R. Nelson of Knoxville, mentioned below.
12. Unidentified.

Chapter 8

1. On Andersonville prison, see Ovid L. Futch, *History of Andersonville Prison* (Tallahassee: Univ. of Florida Press, 1968; *Andersonville* (n.p.: Eastern Acorn Press, 1983). Brownlow's *Knoxville Whig and Revel Ventilator*, Oct. 5, 1864, published an article entitled "Horrible Treatment of Prisoners," which discussed Confederate prisons and featured Andersonville.
2. Sperry, "Diary," in Prindle, *Ancestry of William Sperry Beinecke*, 244. Sperry was one of those sent north (249).
3. The cage is discussed in the Introduction, where RGC's cage-mates are identified as Colonel Dick Morgan and Captain John T. Reynolds.
4. Brigadier General Samuel P. Carter (1819–1891): USA; a native of East Tennessee, and from September 1863 provost-marshal of the region; see

Bryan, "The Civil War in East Tennessee," 123. He was replaced on Jan. 20, 1865 by Lieutenant Colonel Luther S. Trowbridge of the Tenth Michigan Cavalry; *OR* 1.45.2: 620.

5. *The Knoxville Whig and Rebel Ventilator,* Nov. 2, 1864, 2. On Brownlow, E. Merton Coulter, *William G. Brownlow: The Fighting Parson of the Southern Highlands* (1937; Knoxville: Univ. of Tennessee Press, 1971); also Patton, *Unionism and Reconstruction,* 54–57.
6. The Cincinnati and New York accounts have not been located.
7. The *Richmond Enquirer* took the story of RCG's capture and sentencing from the *Knoxville Register* for Oct. 12. Sperry, "Diary" (Prindle, *Ancestry,* 245) also notes that only the threat of Confederate reprisal prevented RGC's execution. *Lex talionis:* law of retaliation.
8. See Bryan, "The Civil War in East Tennessee," 122, 126.
9. These documents are contained in National Archives, Southeast Region (East Point, Ga.), Record Group 21, Minutes, 1864–1868, U.S. District Court, Eastern District of Tennessee, Knoxville, 53A643#92, pp. 79, 178, 237, 238, 321. Archivist Mary Ann Hawkins was kind enough to search out these materials, as well as the records of RGC's treason trial, to be discussed later.
10. Brownlow, *Sketches,* 306.
11. As noted earlier, Breckinridge's wartime papers were destroyed (Munden and Beers, *Guide to Federal Archives Relating to the Civil War,* 136), and I can find no record of these letters. A letter from Breckinridge to Major General S. G. Burbridge, commander of U.S. forces in Lexington, Kentucky, dated Jan. 12, 1865, threatens retaliation if three Confederate officers held there are harmed; *OR* 2.7: 57.
12. Brigadier General John H. Morgan wrote to Carter on Aug. 7, 1864, stating that he held Captain Benjamin Rogers of the Tennessee Union Guard hostage for the safety of Clark's cell mate, Captain Reynolds; *OR* 2.7: 561.
13. It was not unusual for prisoners to receive goods from outside. Sperry, "Diary" (Prindle, *Ancestry,* 245) noted that in the jail yard he saw prisoners receiving packages of clothing and other necessities.
14. Unidentified.
15. None of the correspondence between the generals or between RGC and Carter has been found.
16. Both the Federal prisoners and the conditions are confirmed by Sperry, "Diary" (Prindle, *Ancestry,* 245).
17. Judge Connelly F. Trigg, U.S. District judge of East Tennessee, and a moderate in the internecine struggles of the region, as RGC notes below. He

was appointed to the Federal bench in 1862; Munden and Beers, *Guide to Federal Archives*, 111.

18. There are several articles in this period in *The Knoxville Whig and Rebel Ventilator* condemning official leniency toward Rebels (e.g., Aug. 10, 1864, 2; Aug. 31, 1864, 2). None mentions a specific instance, but all call for swift retribution against Confederates.

19. The exodus is described by Rothrock, ed., *The French Broad-Holston Country*, 145. William J. Kirkham of RGC's Company I was one of those whipped on his return at war's end; Dyer and Moore, *The Tennessee Civil War Veterans Questionnaires*, 3, 1302.

20. Horace Maynard (1814–82), from Worcester County, Mass. He moved to Knoxville in 1838 as a teacher in East Tennessee College, became U.S. congressman in the Whig party, a diplomat, and U.S. postmaster general. See Rothrock, ed., *The French Broad-Holston Country*, 453–54.

21. Thomas Amis Rogers Nelson (1812–73) of Roane County, Tennessee, a distinguished trial lawyer, law partner of Andrew Johnson, Whig member of the U.S. Congress, and judge of the Tennessee Supreme Court. He was also one of RGC's legal counsels at the trial held in 1865. Nelson was a longtime friend of W. G. Brownlow and a Unionist, but moderate in his views of Rebels. See Thomas B. Alexander, *Thomas A. R. Nelson of East Tennessee* (Nashville: Tennessee Historical Commission, 1956).

22. Lieutenant (later Captain) Pleasant Miller McClung (1824–63), son of Charles McClung of Sparta, Tennessee; he was killed in battle at Knoxville on June 20, 1863. See McClung Family Papers at the McClung Historical Collection, and Rothrock, ed., *The French Broad-Holston Country*, 136–37.

23. There is no speech of this nature recorded in the *Congressional Globe* (predecessor of the *Congressional Record*) from 1858 to 1862. The only statement by Maynard related in any way to such ideas is a brief objection of Dec. 31, 1860 to a resolution affirming the Union and its right to defend and preserve itself. Perhaps Maynard made the speech in question elsewhere.

24. Again, no record of the speech could be located.

25. For Judge Trigg, see above, note 17; Colonel John Baxter; Perez Dickinson; James Hervey Cowan; Colonel John Williams; General William C. Kyle of Hawkins County. All were prominent citizens of the region. Trigg and Baxter were lawyers, and they and Kyle were active in politics; Cowan and Dickinson were merchants and RGC's erstwhile employers. See Rothrock, ed., *The French Broad-Holston Country*, passim; and Oliver P. Temple, *East Tennessee and the Civil War* (Cincinnati: Robert Clarke Co., 1899), 171.

26. Identified here as Dr. Charles W. Leonard, an Assistant Surgeon in the

Tenth Michigan Cavalry stationed then at Knoxville, whose residence at the time of his enlistment was Newaygo, Michigan. See John Robertson, *Michigan in the War* (Lansing, Mich.: W. S. George & Co., 1882), 872; my thanks to Arthur Wagner of the Tennessee State Library and Archives, Nashville, for this reference.

27. The date is recorded in the Tennessee State Archives, Military Prison Hospital, Knoxville, Tennessee. Reg. No. 831, Hospital No. 174, p. 5, a reference provided by Gary Clark.
28. The Rev. Dr. James Park (1822–1912), a Presbyterian minister who at this time was principal of the school. See Rothrock, ed., *The French Broad-Holston Country*, 282–83, 464–66.
29. A streptococcal skin infection, it was a common disease among Civil War soldiers; Eaton, *A History of the Southern Confederacy*, 102.
30. Mary Alexander: sister of Major Charles M. Alexander, RGC's friend who had died in Knoxville early in the war.
31. For Nelson and Baxter, see notes 21 and 25, above; Colonel John Netherland was a law partner of Nelson and Andrew Johnson, and was a Whig who sided with the Union (Muriel M. C. Spoden, *Ancestry and Descendants of Richard Netherland, Esquire (1764–1832)*, n.p., 1979). All three were Unionists who favored tolerance in dealing with Rebels after the war, and were among the most distinguished lawyers of East Tennessee.
32. Isabella M. White French, daughter of U.S. Senator Hugh Lawson White and granddaughter of James White, founder of Knoxville. In 1850 she had been in the first class to receive from the East Tennessee Female Institute a degree with the charming title of "Mistress of Polite Literature"; see Creekmore, *Knoxville*, 188.
33. Hugh Lawson White, d. 1840, was elected U.S. senator in 1825; see Stanley J. Folmsbee, Robert E. Corlew, and Enoch L. Mitchell, *Tennessee, A Short History* (Knoxville: Univ. of Tennessee Press, 1969), 168, 187–89; and Cole, *The Whig Party in the South*, 39–41. Henry Clay, Daniel Webster, and John C. Calhoun served in various posts in the U.S. government when White was a senator.
34. William Henry Harrison (1773–1841): the victorious Whig candidate for president in 1840, who died after only a month in office.
35. Ella Cocke: daughter of John Cocke, Jr., a well-to-do citizen of Knox County. She was four years old in 1850, making her about nineteen at the time of this episode; "United States Census 1850 for Knox County, Tennessee," typescript, ed. L. E. Luttrell (for the East Tennessee Historical Society,

1949) 93, and Virginia Webb Cocke, *Cocke, Cockes and Cousins* (Ann Arbor: Edwards Brothers, 1974), 2: 113.

36. In his study of the Tennessee veterans, Fred Arthur Baily found that well-to-do planters and professionals were more likely than those of the working class to refuse the loyalty oath and its offer of freedom; *Class and Tennessee's Confederate Generation*, 99.

Chapter 9

1. Despite numerous searches and inquiries, I have been unable to learn the name of the Federal officer or any particulars of the episode. Brownlow's notice, which is not in the *Whig and Rebel Ventilator,* may have been published as a broadsheet.
2. National Archives, Southeast Region, Record Group 21, Criminal Docket, 1864–1869, U.S. Circuit Court, Eastern District, Tennessee, Knoxville, 53A643#78, p. 238.
3. Andrew Johnson (1808–75), of North Carolina; moved to East Tennessee 1826; served as Tennessee's U.S. congressman, governor, and during most of the war, military governor; U.S. senator, U.S. vice-president under Lincoln, and president after Lincoln's assassination in 1865.
4. George Crosby, of Grainger County, Tennessee, enlisted as a private in Company I in Oct. 1862. He was captured several times, the last, which corresponds to this event, on March 31, 1865 (Compiled Service Records M268, no. 333).
5. For bridge burners, see Seymour, *Divided Loyalties,* 34. "Parson" Brownlow was implicated in the bridge burnings and arrested along with others charged in the episode; only two of the group were hanged.
6. Abner Baker, son of Dr. James Harvey Baker.
7. William Hall, son of M. L. Hall, clerk of the Federal court in Knoxville; "Register of Events and Facts Recorded Annually by David Anderson Deaderick," in *East Tennessee Historical Society Publications* 8 (1936): 73.
8. This event is recounted, also from the Confederate point of view, in Deaderick's "Register," 73, which states that Hall was uncommonly large and Baker quite small, and that Hall began hitting Baker with a stick. Deaderick states that Baker was hanged by a group of ten Tennessee Unionist soldiers, and that none was arrested. "In consequence of this lawless act, and of threats of further violence," he continued, "all the returned rebel soldiers and some others *have gone south.*" The Abner Baker affair is given a different slant in MacArthur, "Knoxville's History: An Interpretation," in *Heart*

of the Valley, ed. Deaderick, 27, which says that Abner accused William Hall of killing the senior Baker, and when Hall denied the charge Baker shot him. Violence of this sort continued through the 1860s; Bryan, "The Civil War in East Tennessee," iv.

9. Bryan, "The Civil War in East Tennessee," 127.
10. National Archives, Southeast Region, Record Group 21, Criminal Docket, 1864–1869, U.S. Circuit Court, Eastern District, Tennessee, Knoxville, 53A643#78, p. 238.
11. Crawford W. Hall, appointed United States Attorney for the Eastern District of Tennessee, March 11, 1865. Steve Cotham of the McClung Historical Collection offered this identification.
12. Robert Kyle, Jr., of Rogersville, Tennessee.
13. John Bell Brownlow (1839–1922), a Lieutenant Colonel in the Ninth Tennessee Cavalry: USA; became editor of the *Whig* when his father was elected governor of Tennessee; Rothrock, ed., *The French Broad-Holston Country*, 386.
14. Judge Trigg's impatience with the Brownlow faction was apparently of long standing. W. G. Brownlow as governor wrote to the *Whig and Rebel Ventilator* a letter, published in the May 31, 1865, issue, complaining that Judge Trigg had wrongfully accused him of mistreating Rebels. The governor's running feud with the more humane Judge Trigg is again reported in an article entitled "Judge Trigg's Court" in the paper's June 21, 1865, issue. No mention is made in the *Whig* of RGC's hearing.
15. The date on which RGC was freed on bond is known from his Compiled Service Record; it is also the date of the final subpoena listed in the Circuit Court records cited above. The date set for the trial is given in the same Circuit Court records.
16. Charles M. McClung: identity uncertain in a large Knoxville family with many members called Charles, and children not always named in the family genealogies.
17. John E. Helms (b. 1828), publisher of the *Knoxville Daily Gazette and Mail*, beginning 1866 (Helms family papers, McClung Historical Collection). Helms was the former business associate of Jacob Austin Sperry ("Diary," Prindle, *Ancestry*, 247).
18. Unidentified.
19. Both unidentified.
20. At the time of RGC's petition for pardon, Johnson's initially rigid attitudes toward Confederate petitioners had softened. On Johnson's policies in these matters, see Jonathan Truman Dorris, *Pardon and Amnesty under Lincoln and Johnson* (Chapel Hill: Univ. of North Carolina Press, 1953), 95–97, 108–114); Lewis R. Gould drew my attention to this reference.

NOTES FOR PAGES 74-80

21. His oath of allegiance and petition for pardon are dated June 19, 1865; the latter was filed July 6, 1865, and executed Oct. 26, 1865; National Archives, Case Files of Applications from Former Confederates for Presidential Pardons 1865–1867, Record Group 94, Tennessee, p. 455; see also 40th Congress, 1st Session, House of Representatives, Report no. 7, Impeachment of the President (serial 1314, p. 1016). My thanks to Marion O. Smith of the Andrew Johnson Project for locating these papers and sending me copies of them. The pardon date is also mentioned in the property rights trial record of June 22, 1866; see above, chap. 7, note 9. For those excluded from pardon, see Dorris, *Pardon and Amnesty under Lincoln and Johnson*, 111.
22. National Archives, Record Group 21, Minute Book B, 1865–1870, U.S. Circuit Court, Eastern District, Tennessee, Knoxville, 53A643#44, case no. 1258.
23. Thomas Berry (1821–1926) had been a captain in the Confederate army and was later a successful businessman of Rome, Georgia. For this and other information on Rome citizens and businesses, I thank Jacqueline D. Kinzer of the Special Collections Department, Rome-Floyd County Library.
24. Perhaps R. J. Johnson, a merchant mentioned in Wade Banister Gassman, "A History of Rome and Floyd County, Georgia in the Civil War" (Master's thesis, Emory Univ., 1966), 82.
25. Unidentified.

EPILOGUE

1. Recorded in a family bible. The daughters were Alice Rosalie (1869–95) and Martha Caroline (1871–1947); a boy and a girl born subsequently died as infants.
2. Daisy King is mentioned in Spencer B. King, *Ebb Tide, as Seen Through the Diary of Josephine Clay Habersham, 1863* (Athens: Univ. of Georgia Press, 1958), 48, 51, 65; she was the diarist's niece.
3. Josephine Habersham (1895–1966), Reuben Grove, Jr. (1896–1968), and Nephew King (1898–1962; the editor's father).
4. In 1896 Reuben Clark gave $3,000, a handsome sum in those days, to build a Sunday School at the church as a memorial to his daughter Rosalie; George Magruder Battey, Jr., *A History of Rome and Floyd County* (Atlanta: Webb and Vary Co., 1922), 493. The building was demolished in more recent times.
5. See *The Tribune of Rome*, October 2, 1888, 46 and *Cherokee Georgia* (Rome, Ga., 1888), 34. The R. G. Clark & Co. building is pictured in *Rome and*

Floyd County. An Illustrated History, 1834–1984 (Rome, Ga.: Sesquicentennial Comm. of the City of Rome, 1985), 96, and in *Cherokee Georgia*, 35. For these and other references in local publications I am grateful to The Rome-Floyd County Library and to Dr. D. J. Wyatt of Rome.

6. *Rome City Directory* (1888), 132–33.
7. Clark's view of the election procedures may have been colored by the scandals surrounding David B. Hill, an important member of Cleveland's party in New York State, and the vigorous and well-funded efforts to foil Hill's candidacy for the governorship. See Allan Nevins, *Grover Cleveland. A Study in Courage* (New York: Dodd, Mead & Co., 1933), 424–25.
8. This letter, written on the letterhead of the Merchants National Bank, R. G. Clark, President, was found in the Cleveland Papers, ser. 2, reel 65, by Lewis L. Gould, who very kindly sent me a photocopy of it. The original spellings and punctuation have been retained.
9. The gift is recorded in a receipt, dated Dec. 15, 1896, from the Southern Express Company for shipping the bird; and in a letter of Jan. 7, 1897, from the president's private secretary expressing Cleveland's "hearty appreciation." Both, in the possession of Josephine Battey Hollingsworth, were found in a book owned by Clark.
10. A typescript statement by Maude H. Yancey of Rome, a family friend. Daisy Clark used to tell of an older Aaron bringing the carriage around to take her and her children to the train to visit her sister Edith (Mrs. James U. Jackson) in Augusta, and that they would usually miss the train. Both anecdotes were related to me by Josephine Hollingworth.
11. The negatives are now in the Georgia Historical Society, Savannah.
12. Noted in an undated letter written by Daisy's mother (in the editor's possession).
13. Will: almost certainly Charles William King, Daisy's brother.
14. John Paul Cooper, whose family lived near the Clarks.
15. In the possession of Josephine Hollingsworth.

APPENDIX

1. *Tennesseans in the Civil War*, 2 vols. (Nashville: Civil War Centennial Commission, 1964), vol. 1: 298–300.
2. The Compiled Service Record of the Fifty-ninth Tennessee is in the National Archives, Record Group 109, microfilm M268, nos. 333–336. Eakin (M268, no. 334) enlisted as a private on Dec. 12, 1861; he took command of the battalion as a major, by Nov. 1862 was listed as a Lieutenant Colonel,

and was promoted to Colonel on March 19, 1863; see also, *Southern Historical Society Papers* 2 (July–Dec., 1876): A98.
3. Pollard, *Southern History of the War*, 374.
4. Compiled Service Records, M268, no. 333. Cooke enlisted Nov. 23, 1861, at age 41 as captain; he was elected colonel on June 30, 1862. More on his military career is noted below.
5. Regimental officers are listed at the beginning of Compiled Service Records, M268, no. 333, and the regiment's history is summarized on printed muster slips. See also *Tennesseans in the Civil War* 1: 298–99, and Lindsley, *The Military Annals of Tennessee. Confederate*, 571–72.
6. Compiled Service Records, M268, passim; see also Dyer and Moore, *The Tennessee Civil War Veterans Questionnaires* 2: 460–61.
7. Compiled Service Records, M268, no. 333, and [Shields], "Reminiscences," 5.
8. Compiled Service Records, M268, no. 333; John B. Shields, in his "Reminiscences," 5, describes the duty in Knoxville. Like most post-war memoirs, his is not without error, and he gives Cooke's rank as colonel.
9. "Capture of Birch Cook," *Knoxville Whig and Rebel Ventilator*, Aug. 10, 1864, 1.; Brownlow, *Sketches*, 354. Brownlow always misspelled Cooke's name.
10. Brownlow, *Sketches*, 354, 359.
11. *Knoxville Whig and Rebel Ventilator*, Aug. 10, 1864, 1; see also "Case of Burch Cook," in the same journal for Aug. 17, 1864, 2, and Coulter, *William G. Brownlow*, 186.
12. OR 1.16.2: 716, 719.
13. The brigade was in the Third Division under Brigadier General Henry Heth; OR 1.16.2: 985.
14. OR 1.16.2: 698.
15. OR 1.16.2: 716 (June 30, 1862).
16. OR 1.16.2: 716; the writer was Adjutant General H. L. Clay.
17. Compiled Service Records, M268, Company I muster roll for Sept. and Oct. 1862; [Shields], "Reminiscences," 5.
18. OR 1.16.2: 773.
19. OR 1.16.2: 779.
20. See Kenneth A. Hafendorfer, *Perryville, Battle for Kentucky* (Utica, Ky.: McDowell Publications, 1981), 12, 86, 90, 98, and Pt. 2. The assessment then and now is that, based on insufficient intelligence about Union troop movements, Bragg failed to concentrate Rebel forces at the right location.
21. Compiled Service Records, M268, no. 333, Company I events slip for Sept.–Oct. 1862.

22. Report of Captain William H. Smith, Company I commander, in the Compiled Service Records, M268, no. 333.
23. *OR* 1.20.2: 453, 466.
24. *OR* 1.24.2: 326, 1.24.3: 612. Reynolds's brigade at Vicksburg was composed of the Third, Thirty-first, Forty-third, and Fifty-ninth Tennessee regiments, the Third Maryland battery, and R. S. Van Dyke's cavalry company.
25. *OR* 1.24.3: 702 and 979.
26. A West Point graduate, Reynolds had served in the U.S. Army, and joined the Confederacy in 1861; John E. Stanchak, article on Reynolds in Faust, ed., *Historical Times Illustrated Encyclopedia*, 625.
27. Compiled Service Records, M268, no. 333. Cooke's letter of resignation is dated Feb. 28, 1863. His ailments, common among troops with poor food and even poorer sanitation, were confirmed by an affidavit from a regimental surgeon.
28. The second enlistment is not recorded in the Compiled Service Record. As noted above, W. G. Brownlow documents his 1864 capture.
29. *OR* 1.24.3: 604, letter from Stevenson to Adjutant and Inspector General W. L. Lovell.
30. *OR* 1.24.1: 656, report by Major General William W. Loring.
31. Bearss, *The Vicksburg Campaign*, 2: 582–84.
32. *Atlas to Accompany the Official Records*, 135-C no. 4, does not show Reynolds's brigade as part of the main battle.
33. The events of the retreat are described in *OR* 1.24.1: 266, 1.24.2: 93–99, 101–108, 143; Carnes, "We Can Hold Our Ground," 27–29; and Bearss, *Decision*, 243–46, 285–86 and *The Vicksburg Campaign*, 2: 629–31.
34. Report by Colonel A. W. Reynolds, *OR* 1.24.2: 107–09. See a lively description of the retreat in Carnes, "We Can Hold Our Ground," 28–29.
35. *OR* 1.24.3: 891–92.
36. *OR* 1.24.2: 93–99.
37. *OR* 1.24.1: 266.
38. Of the 1373 men listed overall in the Compiled Service Record for the Fifty-ninth regiment, 13 percent were captured, and about half of those were taken at Big Black. In Carnes, "We Can Hold Our Ground," 29, Lieutenant Smith mentions the capture of units and men of his Thirty-first Tennessee regiment, also in Reynolds's brigade, during the retreat.
39. Bearss, *Decision*, 290–92 and *The Vicksburg Campaign*, 2: 638–39.
40. *OR* 1.24.2: 355.
41. Johnson and Buel, eds., *Battles and Leaders*, 516; Bearss, *The Vicksburg Campaign*, 3: 888.

42. Bearss, *The Campaign for Vicksburg*, 3: 737.
43. *OR* 1.24.2: 355, report of July 4, 1863, by Colonel A. W. Reynolds on the Siege of Vicksburg.
44. Clement A. Evans, ed., *Confederate Military History*, 12 vols. (Atlanta: Confederate Publishing Co., 1899; reissued New York: Thomas Yoseloff, 1962), vol. 2: 85.
45. Major Samuel H. Lockett, chief engineer of the Vicksburg defenses, quoted in Richard Wheeler, *The Siege of Vicksburg* (1978; New York: Harper, 1991), 229.
46. Bearss, *The Vicksburg Campaign*, 3: 1301.
47. [Shields], "Reminiscences," 6.
48. The account in [Shields], "Reminiscences," 6–7, says that the regiment marched to Enterprise, then to Demopolis, Alabama, and there they were paroled. Shields's statements, written in May 1922, are sometimes inaccurate, and his account of the Vicksburg paroles is a case in point.
49. [Shields], "Reminiscences," 8; confirmed by the muster slips in the Compiled Service Records, M268, nos. 333–36.
50. The long delay between parole and official exchange resulted from President Davis's objections to the terms of the exchange cartel; William Best Hesseltine, *Civil War Prisons* (Columbus: Ohio State Univ. Press, 1930), 69–72.
51. Company F, Record of Events for June 30–Oct. 31, 1863; [Shields], "Reminiscences," 7, which gives the exchange date as Sept. 13.
52. Compiled Service Records, M268, no. 333, Record of Events, Company F, for June 30–Oct. 31, 1863. See also Eakin's letter p. 95.
53. [Shields], "Reminiscences", 7, states that some of Company I were at Bristol, Abington, and Wytheville, Virginia, which probably confuses the period after Vicksburg with that after the 1864 Shenandoah campaign. His placement of the Battle of Morristown (Oct. 28, 1864) just after the Siege of Knoxville (Nov. 29–Dec. 5. 1863) is clearly erroneous.
54. Compiled Service Records, M268, no. 336, where a surgeon's certificate, dated Oct. 17, 1863, states that Smith had been suffering from tuberculosis for a year.
55. Compiled Service Records, M268, no. 333 (RGC).
56. *OR* 1.31.3: 639. The new brigade was put in Carter Stevenson's division in the Army of Tennessee under General Bragg; *OR* 1.32.2: 662.
57. *OR* 1.49.1: 990–91.
58. On Vaughn, see Jeffry D. Wert's biographical entry for him in *Historical Times Encyclopedia*, ed. Faust, 779; B. G. Manard, "Vaughn's Brigade," in

The Military Annals of Tennessee. Confederate, ed. Lindsley, 137; *Tennesseans in the Civil War,* 1: 178–80; and *OR,* passim.

59. *OR* 1.31.3: 581–82.
60. Allen C. Redwood, "The Horsemen in Gray," *Civil War Times Illustrated* 9: 3 (June 1970): 4–8, 45–48. The magazine's editor notes that Redwood, a Confederate cavalryman who served under General Lomax, unfairly criticizes the mounted infantry.
61. *OR* 1.31.1: 255.
62. Major General S. B. Buckner's division; *OR* 1.31.3: 891.
63. As reported by Clark. Colonel Brown enlisted at Madisonville, Tennessee, on Dec. 12, 1861, as captain; promoted to major Dec. 23, 1862, to fill the vacancy left by the death of Major C. M. Alexander, and to lieutenant colonel on March 19, 1863; Compiled Service Records, M268, no. 333.
64. *OR* 1.31.2: 643, 1.32.3: 723.
65. *OR* 1.32.2: 643.
66. Compiled Service Records, M268, no. 334.
67. *OR* 1.32.2: 581, 595-96, 599, 607, 629, 632, 710, 777; 1.32.3: 43, 72, 98, 108, 149, 344, 377.
68. Reuben signed up, among others, Benjamin Tipton at Rogersville on Feb. 18, 1864, and F. Taylor on April 1 of that year; Compiled Service Records, M268, no. 336. Regimental muster slips indicate other enlistments at this time.
69. *OR* 1.32.3: 377, 842–43.
70. *OR* 1.32.3: 803, letter of April 21, 1864, from General S. B. Buckner to Adjutant General Samuel Cooper in Richmond.
71. John D. Imboden, "The Battle of New Market, Va., May 15th, 1864," in Johnson and Buel, eds., *Battles and Leaders,* 4: 485. Imboden says the pickup force numbered less than 4,500, but an editor's note, citing a telegram from Vaughn to Bragg put the figure at 5,600.
72. Vaughn's opposition is noted by Lindsley, *Military Annals of Tennessee, Confederate,* 141.
73. The unit list for Vaughn in Brice, *Conquest of a Valley,* 57, does not mention the Fifty-ninth.
74. *OR* 1.37.1: 95.
75. Eakin was sent to Johnson's Island, Ohio. In May 1865 he wrote to President Johnson, a fellow Tennessean with whom he claimed past acquaintance, requesting release on health grounds and especially "for a wife and three little daughters." In his letter to Johnson, he notes that his two younger brothers served in the Union army. He was finally freed on July 25, 1865. See Compiled Service Records, M268, no. 334.

76. Brice, *Conquest of a Valley*, 79–80.
77. On the gap, see Brice, *Conquest of a Valley*, 61, 73, 79, and Whitehorn, "Piedmont," in *The Civil War Battlefield Guide*, ed. Kennedy, 233.
78. *OR* 1.37.1: 150–51. In a report written that same night at Fishersville, Vaughn says only "The battle was fought today at Piedmont," never mentioning the outcome!
79. *OR* 1.37.1: 150, 151; Brice, *Conquest of a Valley*, 82, 89, 99.
80. See Davis, *Breckinridge, Statesman, Soldier, Symbol*.
81. *OR* 1.37.1: 755.
82. Davis, *Breckinridge*, 439.
83. F. Cooling, *Jubal Early's Raid*, 10. Although he never married, Early had a long relationship with a woman named Julia McNealey in his hometown of Rocky Mount, Virginia; she bore him four children; Charles C. Osborne, *Jubal: The Life and Times of General Jubal A. Early, CSA, Defender of the Lost Cause* (Chapel Hill, N.C.: Algonquin Books, 1992), 31.
84. Randolph H. McKim, *A Soldier's Recollections: Leaves from the Diary of a Young Confederate* (1910; rpt. Washington, D.C.: Zenger, 1983), 226.
85. William C. Davis, "'Jubilee,' General Jubal A. Early," *Civil War Times Illustrated* 9: 7 (Nov. 1970): 11.
86. The best account of Early's life and military career is Osborne's lively and well-documented *Jubal*.
87. David, *Breckinridge*, 440.
88. *OR* 1.51.2: 983, 1020; Davis, *Breckinridge*, 437–38; Early, *Narrative*, 373.
89. *OR* 1.37.1: 765.
90. In a communiqué of 10:30, Breckinridge's adjutant, J. Stoddard, Johnston sought Vaughn's immediate explanation for not following orders (*OR* 1.37.1: 764). Brice, *Conquest of a Valley*, 120, goes so far as to say that Vaughn impeded the defense of Lynchburg by refusing to comply with the order to meet with Hill.
91. Krick, "'The Cause of All My Disasters'," 91; *OR* 1.51: 1020. The Southern press had been merciless in condemning the inaction of Vaughn and Imboden during Crook's charge at Piedmont, and Early seems to have been ready to believe the worst. See Memoir, chap. 6, note 5.
92. Early, *Narrative*, 275–76.
93. Early, *Narrative*, 374.
94. *Atlas to Accompany the Official Records*, 83 no. 7.
95. Brice, *Conquest of a Valley*, 120; Osborne, *Jubal*, 258.
96. Early describes events surrounding the defense of Lynchburg and the subsequent pursuit of Hunter in *Narrative*, 373–79. Osborne, *Jubal*, 252–59, is a good review of this episode.

97. David, *Breckinridge*, 443.
98. Ibid.
99. On Early's commanders in the Shenandoah, see Jeffry D. Wert, "Jubal A. Early and Confederate Leadership," in Gary W. Gallagher, *Struggle for the Shenandoah* (Kent, Ohio: Kent State Univ. Press, 1991), 19–40.
100. Davis, *Breckinridge*, 443.
101. [Shields], "Reminiscences," 8.
102. Davis, *Breckinridge*, 445.
103. Early, *Narrative*, 382–86.
104. On the battle of Monocacy, see Cooling, *Jubal Early's Raid*, 61–81.
105. Cooling, 78.
106. Cooling, 256.
107. Cooling, 70, 74, 256.
108. [Shields], "Reminiscences," 8.
109. Cooling, *Jubal Early's Raid*, 110.
110. On these events, see Cooling, *Jubal Early's Raid*, and Frank E. Vandiver, *Jubal's Raid: General Early's Famous Attack on Washington in 1864* (New York: McGraw Hill, 1960); and on Grant's response, Cooling, *Symbol, Sword, and Shield*, 209.
111. [Shields], "Reminiscences," 8.
112. Early, *Narrative*, 397.
113. [Shields], "Reminiscences," 8.
114. *Atlas to Accompany the Official Records*, 83 no. 6, notes Vaughn "with mounted troops."
115. Early, *Narrative*, 397–98.
116. OR 1.37.1: 171.
117. OR 1.37.1: 286, General Crook's report.
118. Under Brigadier General John H. Morgan; OR 1.39.2: 742. Bradford commanded the Thirty-first Tennessee Regiment. See also [Shields], "Reminiscences," 8.
119. OR 1.37.: 346; Pollard, *Southern History of the War* 2: 400–1.
120. OR 1.37.1.171.
121. Early, *Narrative*, 402; OR 1.43.1: 753.
122. Wert, *From Winchester to Cedar Creek*, 13, 30.
123. Early, *Narrative*, 406; OR 1.43.1: 92, 417–72.
124. Wert, *From Winchester to Cedar Creek*, 34–35.
125. [Jedediah Hotchkiss], *Make Me a Map of the Valley: The Civil War Journal of Stonewall Jackson's Topographer*, ed. Archie P. McDonald (Dallas: Southern

Methodist Univ. Press, 1973), 223. Hotchkiss was now Early's topographic engineer.

126. OR 1.43.1: 1003. Early, *Narrative*, 416, reporting on the period of early September, stated that most of Vaughn's men had already left without permission. This sour comment does not, however, agree with the Compiled Service Records' facts on the periods of high desertion rates and may be only a product of Early's distrust of his cavalry commanders; see Wert, *From Winchester to Cedar Creek*, 25, and Robert K. Krick, "The Cause of All My Disasters," 77–106; the latter, which is undocumented, takes perhaps an overly negative view of Early's cavalry.

127. Brice, *Conquest of a Valley*, 131; Early, *Narrative*, 410; Lindsley, *Military Annals of Tennessee, Confederate*, 142; OR 1.43.1: 572.

128. Bean is identified in the index of OR 1.39.3. Vaughn mentions Bean as commander in a letter of Oct. 17, 1864, to Breckinridge; OR 1.39.1: 848. For Gillespie, of the Forty-third Tennessee, see Lindsley, *Military Annals of Tennessee, Confederate*, 142.

129. Wert, *From Winchester to Cedar Creek*, 39.

130. [Shields], "Reminiscences," 8.

131. Early, *Narrative*, 424.

132. *Atlas to Accompany the Official Records*, 99, no. 1.

133. Wert, *From Winchester to Cedar Creek*, 96; General John B. Gordon, *Reminiscences of the Civil War* (New York: Scribner, 1903), 322.

134. Wert, *From Winchester to Cedar Creek*, 110.

135. OR 1.43.2: 873–76.

136. Wert, *From Winchester to Cedar Creek*, 111, called Early's disposition of Lomax at Winchester "a tactical blunder of the highest order." On Early's distrust of the cavalry, see Osborne, *Jubal*, chap. 15, and Krick, "'The Cause of All My Disasters'."

137. Captain T. B. Beall, "That Stampede at Fisher's Hill," *Confederate Veteran* 5: 1 (January, 1897): 26. Wert, *From Winchester to Cedar Creek*, 119–21, describes the battle and its aftermath; *Atlas to Accompany the Official Records*, 99 no. 2.

138. OR 1.39.3: 819; [Shields], "Reminiscences," 8.

139. OR 1.39.3: 907 and 1.49.1: 1022.

140. OR 1.39.1: 851. The battle is described in Gillem's report, OR 1.39.1: 844–46.

141. Compiled Service Records, M268, no. 336, muster slip for Jan.–Feb. 1865; [Shields], "Reminiscences," 8, who mistakenly puts these events in 1863, after the siege of Knoxville.

142. OR 1.39.1: 892–93; [Shields], "Reminiscences," 9, who describes the ac-

tions of Company I and a company from the Forty-third Tennessee in some detail. See also Lindsley, *Military Annals of Tennessee, Confederate*, 143.
143. [Shields], "Reminiscences," 9.
144. See Vaughn's reports, *OR* 1.39.1: 894–96.
145. Pvt. James Alison Carriger, of Company I, in Dyer and Moore, *The Tennessee Civil War Veterans Questionnaires*, 2: 461.
146. *OR* 1.45.1: 811.
147. *OR* 1.45.1: 835.
148. *OR* 1.45.1: 810–14, General Stoneman's report.
149. *OR* 1.45.1: 834, 1.49.1: 961.
150. [Shields], "Reminiscences," 9.
151. *OR* 1.49.1: 961, 1004. [Shields], "Reminiscences," 8, notes that after the siege of Knoxville, the regiment went to North Carolina "to rest and feed our horses."
152. *OR* 1.49.1: 961, 973–74, 990–91.
153. *OR* 1.49.1: 974.
154. *OR* 1.49.1: 964–65.
155. *OR* 1.49.1: 26.
156. Early, *Narrative*, 466; Osborne, *Jubal*, 390.
157. William J. Kirkham, in Dyer and Moore, *The Tennessee Civil War Veterans Questionnaires*, 3: 1302.
158. [Shields], "Reminiscences," 9. Shields tells an amusing tale of his black servant who furnished the lieutenant with a fine mare by outwitting the Yankee soldiers who had earlier taken Shield's best horse. Shields tarried in Georgia for a second reason: Lieutenant Long's lovely cousin, Carrie E. Long, whom Shields married the following year. For Davis's journey from Richmond, see Burke Davis, *The Long Surrender* (New York: Random House, 1985).
159. *OR* 1.49.1: 30.
160. *OR* 1.49.2: 413–14. The florid account of this episode in Lindsley, *The Military Annals of Tennessee, Confederate*, 144, says that "East Tennesseans, without exception" followed Vaughn.
161. *OR* 1.49.2: 687.
162. The increasing drama of everyday life in Washington is vividly described by Andrews, *The War-Time Journal of a Georgia Girl*, 180–217. See also Davis, ed., *Diary of a Confederate Soldier*, 166–68.
163. *OR* 1.49.2: 685. Eliza Andrews, *War-Time Journal*, 264, describes Captain Abraham as "a big, tall fellow" from Iowa, and, 244, a reasonable, considerate man.
164. *OR* 1.492: 685, 687, 702.
165. *OR* 1.49.2: 623. Abbeville is not far from Washington, Georgia, but

Vaughn was to settle near Thomasville, Georgia.; Wert, entry on Vaughn in *Historical Times Encyclopedia,* ed. Faust, 779.

166. Recorded in the Compiled Service Records, passim.
167. OR 1.32.3: 842–43.
168. Jenifer saddles were designed by Walter H. Jenifer of Baltimore and patented in 1860. They were widely used by officers of both armies during the Civil War. A report of the U.S. Quartermaster Corps also noted that they caused sore backs on the horses. See Randy Steffen, *U.S. Military Saddles 1812–1943* (Norman: Univ. of Oklahoma Press, 1963); Wendy Swik of the Cadet Library, U.S. Military Academy, West Point, furnished this information.
169. Redwood, "The Horsemen in Gray," 48, speaking of the even more severe grain shortages in the Shenandoah Valley in the summer of 1864.
170. OR 1.32.3: 844–45.
171. On sickness in the Confederate army, see Daniel, *Soldiering in the Army of Tennessee,* chap. 5.
172. Daniel, *Soldiering in the Army of Tennessee,* 126–28; Baily, *Class and Tennessee's Confederate Generation,* 94; Bessie Martin, *Desertion of Alabama Troops from the Confederate Army* (New York: AMS Press, 1966), chap. 2, 84–85, 127–34, and passim.
173. When William J. Kirkham, who enlisted in Company I in 1864, reached his native Grainger County, his horse was stolen by "stragglers and bushwackers" who claimed to be Federals, and he was later beaten by men calling themselves Federal soldiers; Dyer and Moore, *The Tennessee Civil War Veterans Questionnaires,* 3: 1302.
174. "Confederates in East Tennessee," *Confederate Veteran* 3 (Sept. 1895): 277.

Bibliography

Alexander, Theodore, et al. *Southern Revenge: Civil War History of Chambersburg, Pennsylvania*. Sheppensburg, Pa.: White Maine and Chambersburg Chamber of Commerce, 1989.
Alexander, Thomas B. *Thomas A. R. Nelson of East Tennessee*. Nashville: Tennessee Historical Commission, 1956.
Amann, William Frayne, ed. *Personnel of the Civil War*. Vol. 1, *The Confederate Armies*. New York: Thomas Yoseloff, 1961.
Andersonville. N.p.: Eastern Acorn Press, 1983.
Andrews, Eliza Frances. *The War-Time Journal of a Georgia Girl, 1864–1865*. Ed. Spencer Bidwell King, Jr. Macon: Ardivan Press, 1960.
Arnold, Louise. *The Era of the Civil War*. Special Bibliographic Series 11. Carlisle Barracks, Pa.: U. S. Army Military History Institute, 1982.
Atlas to Accompany the Official Records of the Union and Confederate Armies. Compiled by Capt. Calvin D. Cowles. Washington: Government Printing Office, 1891–95. Rpt. New York: Thomas Yoseloff, 1958.
Aycock, Roger. *All Roads to Rome*. Rome, Ga.: Rome Area Heritage Foundation, 1981.
Baily, Fred Arthur. *Class and Tennessee's Confederate Generation*. Chapel Hill: Univ. of North Carolina Press, 1987.
Battey, George Magruder, Jr. *A History of Rome and Floyd County*, Atlanta: Webb and Vary, 1922. Rpt. Atlanta: Cherokee Publ., 1969).
Beall, Capt. T. B. "That Stampede at Fisher's Hill," *Confederate Veteran* 5 (1897): 26.
Bearss, Edwin C. "Battle at Champion Hill: Sealing the Fate of Vicksburg," *Strategy and Tactics* 103 (1985): 21–24.
———. *Decision in Mississippi*. Jackson: Mississippi Commission on the War Between the States, 1962.

———. *The Vicksburg Campaign.* 3 vols. Dayton, Ohio: Morningside House, 1986.
Bearss, Edwin C., and Lenard E. Brown. *The Post of Arkansas, 1804–1863.* Washington: Office of History and Historic Architecture, Eastern Service Center, 1971.
Black, Robert C. III. *The Railroads of the Confederacy.* Chapel Hill: Univ. of North Carolina Press, 1952.
Boyer, Reba Bayless, ed. "Marriage Records of McMinn County, Tennessee, 1820–1870." Typescript. McClung Historical Collection, Knoxville.
Bradwell, I. G. "The Battle of Fisher's Hill," *Confederate Veteran* 28 (1920): 338–40.
Brice, Marshall Moore. *Conquest of a Valley.* Charlottesville: Univ. Press of Virginia, 1965.
Brown, D. Alexander. "Battle at Chickasaw Bluffs," *Civil War Times Illustrated* 9: 4 (1970): 4–9, 144–48.
Brownlow, William G. *Sketches of the Rise, Progress and Decline of Secession.* Philadelphia: George W. Childs, 1862. Rpt. New York: Da Capo, 1968.
Bryan, Charles Faulkner, Jr. "The Civil War in East Tennessee: A Social, Political, and Economic Study." Ph.D. dissertation, Univ. of Tennessee, Knoxville, 1978.
———. "'Tories' amidst Rebels: Confederate Occupation of East Tennessee, 1861–63," *East Tennessee Historical Society Publications* 60 (1988): 3.
Campaigns of the Civil War, 8 vols. Vol. 4: Frances Vinton Greene, *The Mississippi* (1882). Vol. 6: George E. Pond, *The Shenandoah Valley in 1864* (1883). Vol. 8: A. T. Mahan, *The Gulf and Inland Waters* (1883). New York: Charles Scribner's Sons. Rpt. New York: Yoseloff, 1963.
Carnahan, J. W. *4000 Civil War Battles from Official Records,* Fort Davis, Tex.: Frontier Book Co., 1971.
Carnes, F. G. "'We Can Hold Our Ground,' Calvin Smith's Diary," *Civil War Times Illustrated* 24: 2 (1985): 24–31.
Carter, Samuel III. *The Final Fortress: the Campaign for Vicksburg 1862–1863.* New York: St. Martin's Press, 1980.
Chesnut, Mary Boykin. *A Diary from Dixie.* Ed. Ben Ames Williams. Boston: Houghton Mifflin, 1949.
Cocke, Virginia Webb. *Cocke, Cockes and Cousins.* 2 vols. Ann Arbor: Edwards Brothers, 1974.
Cole, Arthur Charles. *The Whig Party in the South.* Gloucester, Mass.: Peter Smith, 1962
Commager, Henry Steele, ed. *The Blue and the Gray.* 2 vols. Indianapolis: Bobbs-Merrill Co., 1950.

Connelly, Thomas L. *Civil War Tennessee: Battles and Leaders*. Knoxville: Univ. of Tennessee Press, 1979.

Cooling, Benjamin Franklin. *Jubal Early's Raid on Washington, 1864*. Baltimore: Nautical & Aviation Pub. Co., 1989.

———. *Symbol, Sword, and Shield. Defending Washington during the Civil War*. Hamden, Conn.: Archon, 1975.

Coulter, E. Merton. *William G. Brownlow: the Fighting Parson of the Southern Highlands*. 1937. Rpt. Knoxville: Univ. of Tennessee Press, 1971.

Creekmore, Betsey Beeler. *Knoxville*. Knoxville: Univ. of Tennessee Press, 1958.

Cullen, Joseph P. "The Battle of Winchester." In *Battle Chronicles of the Civil War*, ed. James M. McPherson, vol. 4: 84–96. New York: Collier-Macmillan, 1989.

Cunningham, Edward. *The Port Hudson Campaign, 1862–1863*. Baton Rouge: Louisiana State Univ. Press, 1963.

Daniel, Larry J. *Soldiering in the Army of Tennessee*. Chapel Hill: Univ. of North Carolina Press, 1991.

Davis, Burke. *The Long Surrender*. New York: Random House, 1985.

Davis, William C. *Breckinridge, Statesman, Soldier, Symbol*. Baton Rouge: Louisiana State Univ. Press, 1974.

———, ed. *Diary of a Confederate Soldier: John S. Jackman of the Orphan Brigade*. Columbia: Univ. of South Carolina Press, 1990.

———. "'Jubilee,' General Jubal A. Early," *Civil War Times Illustrated* 9: 7 (Nov. 1970): 4–11, 43–48.

Deaderick, David Anderson. "Register of Events and Facts Recorded Annually by David Anderson Deaderick," 1825–1872. Manuscript, McClung Historical Collection, Knoxville. Partially edited in *East Tennessee Historical Society Publications*, vols. 8 and 9.

Deaderick, Lucile, ed. *Heart of the Valley. A History of Knoxville, Tennessee*. Knoxville: East Tennessee Historical Society, 1976.

Dorris, Jonathan Truman. *Pardon and Amnesty under Lincoln and Johnson*. Chapel Hill: Univ. of North Carolina Press, 1953.

Dyer, G. W., and J. Trotwood Moore, compilers. *The Tennessee Civil War Veterans Questionnaires*. Ed. C. M. Elliott et al. Easley, S.C.: Southern Historical Society Press, 1985.

Early, Jubal Anderson. *A Memoir of the Last Years of the War*. Toronto: C. W. Button, 1867.

———. *Narrative of the War Between the States*. Philadelphia: Lippincott, 1912. Rpt. New York: Da Capo, 1989.

Eaton, Clement. *A History of the Southern Confederacy*. 1954. Rpt. New York: Collier, 1961.

Edmonds, David C. *The Guns of Port Hudson.* 2 vols. Lafayette, La.: Acadiana Press, 1983.
Evans, Clement A., ed. *Confederate Military History.* 12 vols. Atlanta: Confederate Publishing Co., 1899. Rpt. New York: Thomas Yoseloff, 1962.
Faust, Patricia L., ed. *Historical Times Illustrated Encyclopedia of the Civil War.* New York: Harper & Row, 1986.
Fiske, John. *The Mississippi Valley in the Civil War.* New York: Houghton Mifflin, 1900.
Folmsbee, Stanley, Robert E. Corlew, and Enoch L. Mitchell. *Tennessee, A Short History.* Knoxville: Univ. of Tennessee Press, 1969.
Foote, Shelby. *The Civil War. A Narrative.* New York: Random House, 1974.
Freeman, Douglas Southhall. *Lee's Lieutenants.* 3 vols. New York: Scribners, 1942.
Futch, Ovid L. *History of Andersonville Prison.* Tallahassee: Univ. of Florida Press, 1968.
Gallagher, Gary W., ed. *Struggle for the Shenandoah.* Kent, Ohio: Kent State Univ. Press, 1991.
———. "The Shenandoah Valley in 1864." In *Struggle for the Shenandoah,* ed. Gary W. Gallagher, 1–18. Kent, Ohio: Kent State Univ. Press, 1991.
Gassman, Wade Banister. "A History of Rome and Floyd County, Georgia in the Civil War." Master's thesis, Emory Univ., 1966.
Goodspeed's History of Tennessee, 1887, Containing Historical and Biographical Sketches of the Thirty East Tennessee Counties. Nashville: Charles and Randy Elder, 1972.
Gordon, Gen. John B. *Reminiscences of the Civil War.* New York: Charles Scribner's Sons, 1903.
Hafendorfer, Kenneth A. *Perryville, Battle for Kentucky.* Utica, Ky.: McDowell Publications, 1981.
Hale, Will T. *A History of Tennessee and Tennesseans.* 2 vols. New York: Lewis Pub. Co., 1913.
Harper's Pictorial History of the Great Rebellion. 2 vols. Chicago: Star Publishing Co., 1866.
Heiskell, S. G. *Andrew Jackson and Early Tennessee History.* Nashville: Ambrose Printing Co., 1921.
Hesseltine, William Best. *Civil War Prisons.* Columbus: Ohio State Univ. Press, 1930.
Hewitt, Lawrence Lee. *Port Hudson, Confederate Bastion on the Mississippi.* Baton Rouge: Louisiana State Univ. Press, 1987.
Horn, Stanley Fitzgerald. *The Army of Tennessee.* Norman: Univ. of Oklahoma Press, 1953.

Horn, Stanley F., ed. *Tennessee's War 1861–1865 described by Participants.* Nashville: Tennessee Historical Commission, 1965.

[Hotchkiss, Jedediah.] *Make Me a Map of the Valley: The Civil War Journal of Stonewall Jackson's Topographer.* Ed. Archie P. McDonald. Dallas: Southern Methodist Univ. Press, 1973.

Humes, Thomas William. *The Loyal Mountaineers of Tennessee.* Knoxville: Ogden Brothers & Co., 1888.

Imboden, John D. "The Battle of New Market, Va., May 15, 1864." In *Battles and Leaders of the Civil War,* ed. R. U. Johnson and C. D. Buel, 4: 480–86. New York, 1884–1888. Rpt. New York: Yoseloff, 1963.

Johnson, R. U., and C. D. Buel, eds. *Battles and Leaders of the Civil War.* New York, 1884–1888. Rpt. New York: Yoseloff, 1963.

Jones, Katharine M., ed. *Heroines of Dixie: Spring of High Hopes.* 1955. Rpt. New York: Mockingbird, 1974.

Kennedy, Frances H., ed. *The Civil War Battlefield Guide.* Boston: Houghton Mifflin, 1990.

Kennerly, Billie Wyrick. *Tennessee, Grainger County Marriage Bonds and Licenses, 1796–1837.* Vol. 1. Houston: Herb Fisher, n.d.

King, Spencer B. *Ebb Tide as seen through the Diary of Josephine Clay Habersham, 1863.* Athens: Univ. of Georgia Press, 1958.

The Knoxville Whig and Independent Journal. Ed. William G. Brownlow. Knoxville, 1849–1861.

The Knoxville Whig and Rebel Ventilator. Ed. William G. Brownlow. Knoxville, 1863–1865.

Krick, Robert K. "'The Cause of All My Disasters': Jubal A. Early and the Undisciplined Valley Cavalry." In *Struggle for the Shenandoah,* ed. Gary W. Gallagher, 77–106. Kent, Ohio: Kent State Univ. Press, 1991.

Lacy, Eric Russell. *Vanquished Volunteers: East Tennessee and Sectionalism from Statehood to Secession.* Johnson City: East Tennessee Univ. Press, 1965.

———, ed. *Antebellum Tennessee: A Documentary History.* Berkeley: McCutcheon, n.d.

Lash, Jeffrey N. *Destroyer of the Iron Horse. General Joseph E. Johnston and Confederate Railroad Transport, 1861–1865.* Kent, Ohio: Kent State Univ. Press, 1991.

Lewis, Thomas A. *The Shenandoah in Flames.* Alexandria, Va.: Time-Life Books, 1987

Lindsley, John Berrien. *The Military Annals of Tennessee. Confederate.* Series 1. Nashville: J. M. Lindsley, 1886.

Livermore, William Roscoe. *The Story of the Civil War.* 2 vols. New York: G. P. Putnam's Sons, 1913.

Lockett, S. H. "The Defense of Vicksburg." In *Battles and Leaders of the Civil War,* ed. R. U. Johnson and C. D. Buel, 3: 482–92. New York, 1884–1888. Rpt. New York: Yoseloff, 1963.

Long, E. B. *The Civil War Day by Day.* Garden City, N.Y.: Doubleday, 1971.

Lossing, Benson J. *Pictorial History of the Civil War in the United States of America.* 3 vols. Hartford: Thomas Belknap, 1866–1877.

Lucie, Patricia M. L. "Confiscation: Constitutional Crossroads." *Civil War History* 23 (1977): 307–21.

Mahan, A. T. *The Gulf and Inland Waters.* New York: Charles Scribner's Sons, 1888.

Martin, Bessie. *Desertion of Alabama Troops from the Confederate Army.* New York: AMS Press, 1966.

McClung, Rev. William. *The McClung Genealogy.* Pittsburgh: McClung Printing Co., 1904.

McKim, Randolph H. *A Soldier's Recollections: Leaves from the Diary of a Young Confederate.* 1910. Rpt. Washington D.C.: Zenger, 1983.

McPherson, James M. *Battle Cry of Freedom: the Civil War Era.* New York: Ballantine, 1988.

Milligan, John D. *Gunboats Down the Mississippi.* Annapolis: U. S. Naval Institute, 1965.

Moore, John Trotwood, and Austin P. Foster, eds. *Tennessee the Volunteer State.* Chicago: S. J. Clarke, 1923.

Morgan, George W. "The Assault on Chickasaw Bluffs." In *Battles and Leaders of the Civil War,* ed. R. U. Johnson and C. D. Buel, 3: 462–70. New York, 1884–1888. Rpt. New York: Yoseloff, 1963.

Morgan, John. *The Log House in East Tennessee.* Knoxville: Univ. of Tennessee Press, 1990.

Munden, K. W., and H. P. Beers. *Guide to Federal Archives Relating to the Civil War.* Washington: National Archives, 1962.

Nevins, Allan. *Grover Cleveland. A Study in Courage.* New York: Dodd, Mead & Co., 1933.

Official Records of the Union and Confederate Navies in the War of the Rebellion. 31 vols. Washington: Government Printing Office, 1894–1929.

Osborne, Charles C. *Jubal: the Life and Times of General Jubal A. Early, CSA, Defender of the Lost Cause.* Chapel Hill, N.C.: Algonquin, 1992.

Parks, Joseph H. *General Edmund Kirby Smith, C.S.A.* Baton Rouge: Louisiana State Univ. Press, 1954.

Patton, James Welch. *Unionism and Reconstruction in Tennessee 1860–1869.* 1934. Rpt. Gloucester, Mass.: Peter Smith, 1966.

Pemberton, John C. *Pemberton, Defender of Vicksburg.* Chapel Hill: Univ. of North Carolina Press, 1942.
Pollard, Edward A. *Southern History of the War.* New York: C. B. Richardson. 1866. Rpt. New York: Fairfax Press, 1990.
Pond, George S. *The Shenandoah Valley in 1864.* New York: Charles Scribner's Sons, 1883.
Prindle, Paul W. *Ancestry of William Sperry Beinecke.* North Haven, Conn.: Van Dyke Printing Co., 1974.
Redwood, Allen C. "The Horsemen in Gray." *Civil War Times Illustrated* 9: 3 (June 1970): 4–8, 45–48.
Reeve, Felix. *East Tennessee in the War of the Rebellion.* Washington, 1902.
Robertson, John. *Michigan in the War.* Rev. ed. Lansing, Mich.: W. S. George & Co., 1882.
Rome and Floyd County. An Illustrated History, 1834–1984. Rome, Ga.: Sesquicentennial Committee of the City of Rome, 1985.
Rome City Directory. Atlanta: Howard & Dozier, 1888.
Rothrock, Mary U., ed. *The French Broad-Holston County.* Knoxville: East Tennessee Historical Society, 1946.
Scharf, J. Thomas. *History of Western Maryland.* 2 vols. Philadelphia: Louis H. Everts, 1882.
Seymour, Digby Gordon. *Divided Loyalties.* Knoxville: East Tennessee Historical Society, 1963; rev. ed. 1982.
[Shields, John B.] "The Reminiscences of Judge John Brabson Shields (25 Aug. 1840–13 May 1930)." *East Tennessee Roots* 7, no. 1 (1992): 1–17.
Sistler, Byron and Barbara. *Early East Tennessee Marriages.* Vol. 1. Nashville: Byron Sistler & Associates, 1987.
Spencer, James. *Civil War Generals.* New York: Greenwood, 1986.
Spoden, Muriel M. C. *Ancestry and Descendants of Richard Netherland, Esquire (1764–1832).* N.p., 1979.
Stackpole, Edward J. *Sheridan in the Shenandoah.* New York: Bonanza, 1961.
Strode, Hudson. *Jefferson Davis.* 3 vols. New York: Harcourt, Brace and World, 1955, 1959, 1964.
Temple, Oliver P. *East Tennessee and the Civil War.* Cincinnati: Robert Clarke Co., 1899.
Tennesseans in the Civil War. Nashville: Civil War Centennial Commission of Tennessee, 1964. Rpt. Knoxville: Univ. of Tennessee Press, 1985.
"United States Census 1850 for Knox County, Tennessee." Ed. L. E. Luttrell. Knoxville: East Tennessee Historical Society, 1949.

The War of the Rebellion: a Compilation of the Official Records of the Union and Confederate Armies. 128 vols. Washington: Government Printing Office, 1880–1901.

Vandiver, Frank E. *Jubal's Raid: General Early's Famous Attack on Washington in 1864.* New York: McGraw-Hill, 1960.

———. *Their Tattered Flags: the Epic of the Confederacy.* New York: Harper and Row, 1970.

Van Dyke, Thomas Nixon. "The Van Dyke Genealogy." Typescript, Library of Congress, Washington D.C., and Rome–Floyd County Library, Rome, Ga.

Wert, Jeffry D. "Fisher's Hill." In *Battle Chronicles of the Civil War,* ed. James M. McPherson, vol. 4: 97–107. New York: Collier-Macmillan, 1989.

———. *From Winchester to Cedar Creek: The Shenandoah Campaign of 1864.* New York: Simon & Schuster–Touchstone, 1987.

———. "Jubal A. Early and Confederate Leadership." In *Struggle for the Shenandoah,* ed. Gary W. Gallagher, 19–40. Kent, Ohio: Kent State Univ. Press, 1991.

Wheeler, Richard. *The Siege of Vicksburg.* New York: Harper Perennial, 1978, 1991.

Williams, Thomas J. C. *A History of Washington County Maryland.* Hagerstown, 1906. Rpt. Baltimore: Regional Publishing Co., 1968.

Winters, John D. *The Civil War in Louisiana.* Baton Rouge: Louisiana State Univ. Press, 1963.

Wyatt-Brown, Bertram. *Honor and Violence in the Old South.* New York: Oxford Univ. Press, 1986.

Index

(All military personnel are listed by their highest known rank.)

Abbeville, S.C., 109–10
Abraham, Capt. Lot (USA), 110
Alexander, Maj. Charles M., 13, 67, 86
Alexander, Frances, 67
Alexander, Mary, 64, 67
Anderson, Brig. Gen. Robert (USA), 9
Andersonville Prison, 53–54, 58
Averell, Brig. Gen. William W. (USA), 103, 104

Baker, Abner, 70
Banks, Maj. Gen. Nathaniel P. (USA), 125 n. 3
Barton, Alvin, 75
Barton, Brig. Gen. Seth M. (CSA), 91
battles
—Arkansas Post (Ark.), 14, 16
—Big Black River (Miss.), 22, 91
—Champion Hill (Miss.), 21, 89, 90–91
—Chickamauga (Ga.), 27
—Chickasaw Bluff (Miss.), 14, 89
—First Manassas (First Bull Run; Va.), xxii, 11–12
—Fisher's Hill (Va.), 39–41, 97
—Fort Saunders, Knoxville (Tenn.), 29, 94
—Fort Sumter (S.C.), 9
—Lynchburg (Va.), 33, 97, 100–1
—Monocacy (Relay Station; Md.), 34, 102
—Morristown (Tenn.), 50–51, 106
—Perryville (Ky.), 13, 88
—Piedmont (Va.), xxiv, 30–31, 97–98
—Port Gibson (Miss.), 19–20, 89–90
—Port Hudson (La.), 16
—Richmond (Ky.), 88
—Second Kernstown(Va.), 36, 97, 103
—Third Winchester (Opequon Creek; Va.), 36–38, 97, 105–6
—Vicksburg, xxiii, xxx, 16–24; Confederate surrender at, 92–93; siege of, 23–24, 92–93
Baxter, Col. John (USA), 62, 65, 75
Bean, Lt. Col. Onslow (CSA), 39, 105–6
Beauregard, Brig. Gen. Pierre Gustave Toutant (CSA), 9
Beeler, Pvt. Enoch (CSA), xxx, 41
Bell, John (presidential candidate), 8
"Belle Vue" (Clark family home), 82
Berry, Thomas, 76
Bradford, Col. William M. (CSA), 103
Breckinridge, Maj. Gen. John C. (CSA), 8, 31–33, 36, 38, 55, 57, 63, 64, 89, 99–102, 105–6, 108–9; description of, 98
Bragg, Gen. Braxton (CSA), 13, 88
bridge burning, xxviii, 87, 102
Brown, Lt. Col. James P. (CSA), 86, 95
Brownlow, Lt. John Bell (USA), 13
Brownlow, William Gannaway ("Parson"), xxiv–xxvi, 29, 51, 54–57, 59–60, 62, 65, 70–73, 75, 87, 135 n. 21
Buckner, Maj. Gen. Simon B. (CSA), 26
Burbridge, Maj. Gen. Stephen G. (USA), 134 n. 11
burials, 16, 24–25
Burnside, Maj. Gen. Ambrose (USA), xvii, 26, 29

INDEX

Calhoun, John Caldwell, 10
Carroll, Brig. Gen. William H. (CSA), 118 n. 34
Carter, Col. James E. (CSA), 51
Carter, Brig. Gen. Samuel P. (USA), xxv, 54, 56–58, 62
Chambersburg, Pa., 35
Chestnut, Mary Boykin, 131 n. 61
churches, 11
Clark, Alice Rosalie, 3, 82, 139 n. 1
Clark, John, 69
Clark, Joseph, xviii, 29
Clark, Martha Caroline, 3, 82, 83, 139 n. 1
Clark, Martha Grove, xviii, 5, 29, 69
Clark, Mary Josephine ("Daisy") King, 77, 79, 82–83, 140 n. 10
Clark, Capt. Reuben Grove, ii, 53–76, 78; as author, xviii, xxiii–xxiv, xxx–xxxi; as businessman, xix–xx, 6, 56–57, 74–77, 80; capture of, 51–52; character of, xxx; comments on the military, xxx, 21–22, 24, 37, 48, 50, 53, 92; death of, 84; description of, xxii; early history of, xviii–xxii, 5–6; legal problems of, xxiv–xxvi, 56–57, 69; pardoned, 74–75; and politics, 8–10, 52, 80–82; as prisoner, xxiv–xxix; promotions of, xxiii, 17, 27, 93
Clark, Samuel, xix–xx
Clark, Susan Alice Smith, 77
Clark, Susan Latham, 116 n. 7
Cleage, Thomas, 27
Cleveland, Grover, 80–82
Cobb, John B. (CSA), 85
Cocke, Ella, 67
Company I. *See* Fifty-ninth Tennessee Mounted Infantry Regiment
Confederate Veterans' Assn. of Upper East Tennessee, 113
Conscript Act of April 16, 1862, 86, 112
Cooke, Col. James Burch (CSA), 12, 85–89; and W. G. Brownlow, 87
Cooper, John Paul, 84
Cooper, Adj. Gen. Samuel (CSA), 94
Cowan, James Hervey, 62, 75, 119 n. 2
Cowan, Lucy (Mrs. Charles M. Alexander), 13
Cowan and Dickinson Co. (Knoxville), xx, xxi, xxii, 6, 75
Crawford, R. A., 75
Crook, Maj. Gen. George (USA), 30, 36, 38, 41, 98, 103, 106
Crosby, Pvt. George (CSA), 69

Davis, Jefferson Finis, 9, 21, 69, 91, 94, 109–10
Democratic party, 8–9
Dent, Aaron, 82
desertion, 25, 95, 112
Dickinson, Perez, 58, 62, 75, 119 n. 2
Douglas, Stephen A., 9

Eakin, Maj. William L. (CSA), 12, 14, 31, 85–86, 88, 90, 95–96, 98
Early, Lt. Gen. Jubal A. (CSA), xxiv, 33–35, 36, 38–39, 41, 47, 100 and passim; description of, 99
Early's raid on Washington, xxiv, 35, 97, 101–2
East Tennessee: animosities in, xvii, xxvi, 50, 52, 58–60, 69, 70, 149 n. 173; economy of, xvi; education in, xix; factionalism in, xvii; farming in, xvii–xviii; house types of, xviii, 116 n. 9; slavery in, xvi, xviii
Echols, Brig. Gen. John (CSA), 94, 102, 108–9
Ellet, Col. Charles Rivers (USA), 123 n. 39
Elzey, Brig. Gen. Arnold (CSA), 10–11, 101
engagements and skirmishes: Athens (Tenn.), 108; Bunker Hill (W. Va.), 104; Cove gap (W. Va.), 34, 101; Greenville (Tenn.), 107; Hagerstown (Md.), 103; Lick Creek (Tenn.), 107; Loudon (Tenn.), 94; Marion (Va.), 107; Martinsburg (W. Va.), 44, 101; New Castle (Va.), 34, 101; New Town (Va.), 35–36, 103; Russellville (Tenn.), 107; Salem (Va.), 33; Sweet Sulphur Spring (W. Va.), 34, 101; White Post–New Town Road (Va.), 104; Williamsport (Md.), 35; Wytheville (Va.), 107

Farragut, Adm. David G. (USN), 14
Faulkner, Charles J., 45
Fifty-ninth Tennessee Mounted Infantry Regiment, xxvi, 14, 26–27, 36, 38, 95, 101, 103, 104, 106; and W. G. Brownlow, 87; brigaded, 89; history of, Appendix; formed, 12, 87; management problems in, 95–97, 110–13; mounted, 32, 93, 95–96; valor of, 92
—Company I, xxiii; 13, 27, 43, 93, 94, 107, 109; formed, 12, 86
Fleming, John M., 75
French, Isabella M. White, 66

INDEX

Gammon, Capt. Ed (CSA), 49
Georgia: Athens, 109, 110; Chickamauga, 27; Dalton, 13, 26–27, 93, 95, 96; Decatur, 26; Lexington, 109; Rome, xxx, 44, 49, 75, 77, 80, 113; Washington, 109–10
Geisler, Maj. Henry D. (CSA), 85, 86
Gill, Samuel, 6
Gillem, Brig. Gen Alvan C. (USA), 50–51, 107
Gillespie, Col. James W. (CSA), 105
Goforth, Major, superintentent of East Tenn. and Va. RR, xxvi
Grant, Gen. Ulysses S. Grant (USA), xxx, 19–21, 23–25, 90, 92–93
Gray, Maj. John (USA), 29, 55–56, 72

Hager, Jonathan, 46–47
Hall, Col. Crawford W., 72–73
Hall, William, 70
Hardin, Peter H., 77
Hardin and Johnson Co. (Rome, Ga.), 76, 77, 80
Harris, Gov. Isham G., xvii
Harrison, William Henry, 66
Hawes, Gov. Richard C., 88
Hays, Maj. Jacob M. (CSA), 30
Hazen, G. M., 75
Heiskell, William, 75
Helmes, John E., 74
Hickle, 2nd Lt. Samuel (CSA), 43, 86
Hill, Lt. Gen. Ambrose Powell (CSA), 11
Hill, Maj. Gen. D. Harvey (CSA), 100
Hill, David B., 140 n. 7
Hollingsworth, Josephine Battey, xxxi
Hunter, Maj. Gen. David (USA), 30, 32–36, 101
Hunter, Sen. Robert Mercer Taliaferro, 46

Imboden, Brig. Gen. John D. (CSA), 30, 97–99, 104
iron cage, xxvi–xxix, 54, 58

Jackson, Lt. Gen. Thomas J. Jackson, 29, 37
Jenifer saddles, 111
Johnson, Andrew, 69, 74
Johnston, Gen. Joseph E. (CSA), 10, 21, 26, 37, 90, 96, 109
Jones, Brig. Gen. William E.(CSA), xxiv, 30–31, 98

Kentucky campaign, 88–89, 112
King, Anna Wylly Habersham, 77
King, Rev. Charles Barrington, 77
King, Charles William, 83
King, Edith B. (Mrs. James U. Jackson), 140 n. 10
King, 2nd Lt. James M. (CSA), 47
Kirkham, William J., xix, 149 n. 173
Knoxville County Jail, xxvi–xxix, 54, 87
Knoxville law courts, 56–57, 59, 60, 71–73, 74
Knoxville Whig and Rebel Ventilator, The, xxi, 29, 54, 73
Kyle, Robert, Jr., 72
Kyle, Gen. William C. (USA), 62, 75

Lamont, Daniel S., 81–82
last Confederate encampment, 110
Lee, Gen. Robert E. (CSA), 33, 99, 101, 103, 108
Lee, Comm. S. P. (USN), 16
Leonard, Dr. Charles W. (USA), 62–65, 68
Lincoln, Abraham, 8–10, 69
Lomax, Maj. Gen. Lunsford Lindsay (CSA), 41, 104, 106
Long, Carrie E., 148 n. 158
Long, Pvt. Daniel Wesley (CSA), 43
Long, 2nd Lt. William H. (CSA), 86, 109, 148 n. 158
Longstreet, Lt. Gen. James, 29, 94–96
Loring, Maj. Gen. William W. (CSA), 21–22
Lossing, Benson J., xxviii
Love, Maj. James F. (CSA), 86
loyalty oath, 60, 61, 74
Luttrell, James C., 75

McCarty, Corp. James Croft (CSA), 40
McCausland, Brig. Gen. John (CSA), 35
McClellan, Maj. Gen. George B. (USA), 37
McClerndon, Brig. Gen. John A. (USA), 14
McClung, Charles M., 73
McClung, Pleasant Miller, 61
McNealey, Julia, 145 n. 83
Martin, Maj. Gen. William T. (CSA), 95
Maryland: Hagerstown, 35, 46–48, 103; Monocacy, 34, 102; Williamsport, 35
Maynard, Horace, 60–62
Mayo, George, 56–57
Merchants National Bank, Rome, Ga., 80
Merritt, Maj. Gen. Wesley (USA), 38

military training, xxiii, 86
military units, Confederate
—Fifth Brigade (T. H. Taylor's), 87
—Fifty-ninth Tennessee Mounted Infantry Regiment. *See* Fifty-ninth Tennessee Mounted Infantry Regiment
—First Battalion Tennessee Infantry, 12, 86
—First Battalion Tennessee Volunteers, 86
—First Division, Dept. of Mississippi and East Louisiana (Carter L. Stevenson's), 87, 92
—First Maryland Regiment, 11
—Fourth Brigade, Army of the Shenandoah (1861), 10–11
—Fourth Brigade, Stevenson's Division (A. W. Reynolds's), 87, 89, 90, 93
—Second Virginia Cavalry Regiment, xxiv
—Sixty-fourth North Carolina Regiment, 118 n. 32
—Third Brigade (Alfred Cumming's), Stevenson's Division, 92
—Third Tennessee Infantry Regiment (Vaughn's), xxii, 11, 92, 93
—Thirteenth Virginia Regiment, 11
—Thirty-ninth Tennessee Regiment, 92
—Vaughn's Brigade, Army of Northern Virginia, 93 and passim; management problems in, 108
military units, Union
—Second Ohio Regiment, 108
—Seventh Tennessee Mounted Infantry Regiment, 108
—Eighth Corps, 105
—Eighth Tennessee Regiment, 107
—Tenth Michigan Cavalry Regiment, 110
Mississippi: Bovina, 91; Bridgeport, 91; Chunky Creek, 112; Port Gibson, 19–20; Vicksburg, *see* Vicksburg campaign, *and* battles: Vicksburg; Warrenton, 18, 90
Montgomery, Frederick, telegraph operator, xxvii
Morgan, Col. Dick (CSA), xxvii
Morgan, Brig. Gen. John H. (CSA), 57, 118 n. 32, 146 n. 118
Mulford, Lt. Col. John E., Agent of Exchange (USA), xxviii

Nashville Press and Times, 73
Nelson, Lt. D. M. (USA), 52
Nelson, Thomas A. R., 61, 64
Netherland, Col. John, 65, 72

North Carolina: Charlotte, 109; Mount Airy, 108; Newton, 110

Ore, 1st Sgt. Reese (CSA), 86
Ould, Robert, Agent of Exchange (CSA), xxviii–xxix, 64

Park, Rev. Dr. James, 63
Parsons, Col. Joseph H. (USA), 51–52
Pemberton, Brig. Gen. John C. (CSA), 21–24, 89, 90, 91
Perry, uncle of Brig. Gen. S. P. Carter, 58
Porter, Rear Adm. David D. (USN), 14, 16–19, 122 n. 27
Presbyterians, xviii, xxvi, 48
presidential election 1860, 8
prisoners-of-war: exchange of, xxviii–xxix, 53, 118 n. 36; parole of, 26, 53, 93, 110, 126 n. 1; treatment of, xxvi–xxix, 53–54, 58–59, 134 n. 13

R. G. Clark and Co. (Rome, Ga.), 77
railroads, xvi, xx, xxvii, 26, 27, 33, 38, 101, 102, 112
Ramseur, Maj. Gen. Stephen D. (CSA), 35, 38, 103, 105
Ransom, Maj. Gen. Robert (CSA), 95–97, 100
Republican party, 8
retaliation policy, xxvii, 55–58, 68
Reynolds, Brig. Gen. Alexander W. (CSA), 14, 15, 22, 24, 89–92
Reynolds, Capt. John (CSA), xxvii–xxix, 64
Richmond Enquirer, The, 55
Rodes, Maj. Gen. Robert E. (CSA), 35, 38, 104
Russell, Rev. W. T. (CSA), 86

Sale, Col. John B. (CSA), 111
Schley, Col. George (CSA), 46, 48
Schley, Mary Sophia Hall, 46
Schley, Miss, 46
scorched earth policy, 34, 41
Shenandoah Valley Campaign (Second), xxiii, 30–49, 97–106
Sheridan, Maj. Gen. Philip H. (USA), 36, 38–40, 42, 104–5
Sherman, Maj. Gen. William T. (USA), 109
Shields, Capt. John B. (CSA), 86, 102–3, 105, 107, 109, 148 n. 158
sickness, 25, 64

Smith, Asahel R., 77
Smith, Lt. Gen. Edmund Kirby (CSA), 12, 85
Smith, Maj. Gen. Martin Luther (CSA), 14
Smith, Mary, 27, 126 n. 10
Smith, Brig. Gen. Thomas (CSA), 102
Smith, Capt. William H. (CSA), xxiii, 17, 27, 85–88, 93
Sneed, Col. William H., 51
social class, xvii, xxi, 7, 65
Sperry, Jacob Austin, xxvi
Stevenson, Maj. Gen. Carter L. (CSA), 12, 14, 22, 24, 87–91
Stolsworth, 2nd Lt. Thomas (CSA), 86
Stoneman, Maj. Gen. George (USA), 107
Strick, Rev. Samuel (CSA), 86

Tedcastle, A. W., 77
Tennessee: Athens, 27, 94, 108; Bean Station, 6, 86, 96; Bethel Spring, 86; Blountsville, 96; Bristol, 74, 96, 106, 108, 111; Bull's Gap, 50, 96, 107; Campbell's Station, 29; Cumberland Gap, 96; Elizabethton, 69; Flat Creek, 88; Grainger Co., xvii, xxiii; Greeneville, 107, 109–10; Hawkins Co., xxiii; Horse Creek, 107; Kingsport, 96; Knoxville, xvi, xx, xxii, 6, 26, 88; Lenoir City, 13, 89; Lick Creek, 107; Loudon, 27, 88, 94; Mont Vale Springs, 26, 75–76; Morristown, xxii, xxiv, 10, 50, 52, 88, 106–7; Mossy Creek (Jefferson City), 52, 107; Noes Ferry, 12, 88; Russellville, 107; Rutledge, xviii, xx, 5, 6; Strawberry Plains, 12, 87, 88; Sweet Water, 93, 94, 108; Tazewell, 13, 89, 96
Terry, Brig. Gen. William (CSA), 45
Thomas, Maj. Gen. George H. (USA), 27
Tilghman, Brig. Gen. Lloyd (CSA), 20, 22
Tipton, Pvt. Benjamin (CSA), 144 n. 68
Torbert, Maj. Gen. Alfred T. A. (USA), 104
Tracy, Brig. Gen. Edward D. (CSA), 20, 90
Trigg, Judge Connelly F., 59, 62, 71–73
Trigg, Ed, U.S. Marshall, 59, 69

USS "Albatross," 18
USS "Desoto," 18
USS "Hartford," 18–19
USS "Lancaster," 19

USS "Queen of the West," 17–18
USS "Switzerland," 18–19

Van Dyke, Capt. John (CSA), 43, 49
Van Dyke, Margaret Josephine (Mrs. Hugh Inman), 44
Van Dyke, Mary Hamilton (Mrs. George Battey), 44
Van Dyke, Penelope S., 126 n. 8
Van Dyke, Maj. Richard S. (CSA), 44
Van Dyke, Robert D., 44
Van Dyke, Judge Thomas Nixon, 27, 44, 126 n. 10
Van Dyke, W. D. (CSA), 86
Van Dyke family, 113
Vaughn, Brig. Gen. John C. (CSA), xxiv, xxix, 10, 27, 28, 30–32, 40, 48, 50–51, 86, 89, 93–94, 97, 98, 100
Vicksburg campaign, xxiii, 13–25, 89–93
Virginia: Appomattox, 108; Berryville, 104; Charlottesville, 31, 99; Christiansburg, 109; Darksville, 43–44; Fisher's Hill, 38, 104–5; Harrisonburg, 41, 106; Hillsville, 108; Lynchburg, 32–33, 44; Manassas, 37; Marion, 107; Munson's Hill, 12; New Castle, 101; New Town, 35, 103; Piedmont, 30, 97–98; Rockfish Gap, 32, 98–99, 100; Saltville, 29; Staunton, 30, 43, 97, 101; Stephenson's Depot, 38, 105; Winchester, 11, 35–38, 103, 104–5; Wytheville, 26, 106–7
Virginia Military Institute, 100

Wallace, Maj. Gen. Lewis (USA), 34, 102
Washington, D.C., xxiii–xxiv; Early's raid on, 35, 101–2
West, Sgt. Samuel (CSA), 36
West Virginia: Martinsburg, 36, 44–46, 101, 103; Old Sweet Springs, 83; Sweet Sulphur Springs, 101
Wharton, Maj. Gen. John A. (CSA), 99, 101
Wheeler, Maj. Gen. Joseph (CSA), 108
Whig party, xx, 8–9, 66
White, Hugh Lawson, 66
Williams, Col. John (USA), 62, 75
Williams, Brig. Gen. John S. (CSA), 93
Wright, Josiah I. (CSA), 85

www.ingramcontent.com/pod-product-compliance
Lightning Source LLC
Chambersburg PA
CBHW030322080526
44584CB00012B/664